ALSO BY SUSAN ROANE

How to Work a Room®
The Secrets of Savvy Networking
What Do I Say Next?
RoAne's Rules: How to Make the RIGHT Impression
How to Create Your Own Luck

FACE to FACE

How to Reclaim the Personal Touch in a Digital World

Susan RoAne

A FIRESIDE BOOK
Published by Simon & Schuster
New York   London   Toronto   Sydney

Fireside
A Division of Simon & Schuster, Inc.
1230 Avenue of the Americas
New York, NY 10020

Copyright © 2008 by Susan RoAne

All rights reserved, including the right to reproduce this book or portions thereof in any form whatsoever. For information address Fireside Subsidiary Rights Department, 1230 Avenue of the Americas, New York, NY 10020

First Fireside trade paperback edition October 2008

FIRESIDE and colophon are registered trademarks of Simon & Schuster, Inc.

For information about special discounts for bulk purchases, please contact Simon & Schuster Special Sales at 1-800-456-6798 or business@simonandschuster.com

Designed by Jan Pisciotta

Manufactured in the United States of America

10   9   8   7   6   5   4   3   2   1

Library of Congress Cataloging-in-Publication Data

RoAne, Susan.
   Face to face: how to reclaim the personal touch in a digital world / Susan RoAne.
      p. cm.
Includes index.
1. Business communication. 2. Business networks. 3. Interpersonal communication. 4. Interpersonal relations. I. Title.
HF5718.R58 2008
650.1'3—dc22   2008003315

ISBN-13: 978-1-4165-6142-2
ISBN-10: 1-4165-6142-0

To Joyce (Mumsy) Siegel, Carl LaMell, and Lana Teplick.

Because of you, I am.

ACKNOWLEDGEMENTS

The best part of writing a book is the opportunity to acknowledge those people who "aided and abetted" the process, the book and me. Writing in and of itself, is a solitary endeavor, but I was never really alone.

Those who were always there for me gave me the room to withdraw and become my author alter ego, "Esther Sequester." And they allowed me to drop in as chapters were finished or the muse took a break.

First of all, an incredible thank-you to each and every person who graciously shared their stories, thoughts and experiences. You will get to know them as they are included in this book. Many thanks to those who heard the title and concept of this book and said, "Great idea," or "Much needed." You fueled me.

Literally, so did Andrew and the gang at Café Z, who made sure I had my Belgian waffles and then let me sit for hours, refilling my coffee cup as I wrote "al fresco." Thank you, also, to the team at Fifi's Diner in Bon Air, who made sure my french fries were cooked to crispy perfection.

To Leigh Bohmfalk, who helped me shape this book and offered her insights and suggestions.

To Mary Haring, who added her experiences and thoughts and edited the draft to be sure Face to Face (F2F) wasn't one-generation dimensional.

To Becky Gordon, who not only input from the pencil draft and actually read my writing, but who also shaped, edited, revised and guided the book and me. Thank you for all that you've done, your diligence and your laughter. I couldn't have done it without you!

To Mumsy, Carl and Lana, because they are my pillars.

To Connie Glaser, cosmic soul sister, whose friendship and support mean the world to me.

To Arlynn Greenbaum, who has given me a safe haven in New York and years of friendship.

There are those whose stories you will read and others whose support has been purely joyful: Jean Miller, Toni Boyle, Judith Briles, Patricia Fripp, Diane Parente, Diane Bennett, Laura Fenamore, Kathleen Korth, Barry and Barbara Wishner, Christina Owens, Ira Rosenberg, Marcie Bannon, Jody Pilka, Gert Gurd, Shelly Berger, Bonnie Katz, Robert Spector, Gail Edenson, Mark Chimsky, Griggs RoAne, Susan Belling, Sandy Hufford, Donna Schaefer, Inez Sun Kelly, Ron Buono, Carla Elkins, neighbor and friend, and Aunt Milly Cohen for her unyielding support and belief in me.

Thanks to the team who kept me fit: Sherwood and Jonathan Cummins and Heather Neeley—all of whom who listened to me talk through the book week after week and gave wonderful feedback. To my clients who have been supportive of my writing and shared their "personal touch in this digital world" stories—thank you.

To my families: the Skovs, the Berringers, and the Walkers, for including me in their lives.

And thank you to the transgressors of good taste, whose deeds, actions and behaviors in the shared space also helped shape this book.

To my editor and longtime friend, the wonderful Zach Schisgal, who believed in this book and the value Face to Face offers to readers. I always said that working with him again would be a dream come true. And it has been. What more could an author want?

A special thank you to Shawna Lietzke, Zook's editorial assistant, for her support, and enthusiasm and kindnesses.

And to my dear agent, Michael Bourret—oh, how I wish you were with me on my entire journey as an author and how grateful I am that you're now my agent. Your wisdom, savvy and know-how are matched by your profound support, kindness and wickedly funny sense of humor. Lucky me to have you on my side and in my life.

Thank you to the publicity department, marketing team and sales reps for Fireside, who work so hard to be sure books are in stores. To the bookstore staffs, buyers and hand-sellers, thank you, merci beaucoup, todah rabah, muchas gracías for over nineteen years of your support, efforts, energy and for always being so nice to me as I popped in your stores to autograph books during my walks around your cities.

And to you—the book buyers who spread the word—a special thank you. Without you, I wouldn't be a bestselling author.

CONTENTS

Chapter Nine
Group Gusto: New and Old Ways to Gather Together
000

Chapter Ten
Stand and Deliver: Speeches, Toasts and Introductions
000

Chapter Eleven
Ethical Endings and Exceptional Exits in Real Space
000

Chapter Twelve
Much Ado About Mentors   000

Chapter Thirteen
The Grapevine Is a Goldmine—Redux   000

Chapter Fourteen
Sticky Situations   000

Chapter Fifteen
Techie Toys: Gizmos, Gadgets, and Good Behavior
000

Chapter Sixteen
Route 66: Face-to-Face Steps to Success 000

Afterword   000

RoAne's Readers Guide 000

Index   000

Desperately Seeking Susan   000

PREFACE

f I had to describe the communication skills needed in today's global economy, it would sound like an order in a restaurant: "Surf & Turf, please." We need to be able to surf and use the Internet, be technically adept with use of the gizmos and gadgets of technology and have online skills, whether to research, stay informed, keep in touch or shop. Even I, a self-described "technoyutz," can e-mail photos from my Treo. Don't ask how long it took me to learn! In addition, when we're on the same turf, in the face-to-face space, we need to be equally facile, comfortable, and communicative. That's how we build the common bonds of business and forge our friendships.

Those leaders who understand and implement a memorable personal touch in their interpersonal interactions stand out from the crowd. They're enjoyable, employable and promotable, because they manage the face-to-face communication required in job interviews, presentations, and meetings with coworkers, employees, customers and vendors. And their social lives benefit from their ability to converse, connect and relate face to face.

While we live in a digital world with GPS systems that talk to us and tell us where to go (directionally, that is) and phones that tell us the latest stock market quotes, we crave the old-fashioned personal touch. The rise of crafts (knitting, quilting, woodworking) has been attributed to our need to stay connected to products that have been handmade. Whether it's hand-finished furniture or accessories or gardens, we want that which is home-grown or homemade. The growth of the do-it-yourself industry and the proliferation of farmers' markets in urban areas are examples of our desire for the homegrown, a facet of personal touch. Stationery stores are still in the business of helping us stay in touch by providing cards, personalized notepaper, and good pens with which to write, not type, messages that are personal, remembered, and reread.

My first two books, How to Work a Room® and The Secrets of Savvy Networking, launched an industry about connecting. Our incredible technical advances have given us better and faster ways to communicate and, unfortunately, additional ways to miscommunicate. Face to Face provides guidelines to blend the offline and the online so that we can embrace the opportunity to shine in every in-person, interpersonal interaction.

INTRODUCTION

Congratulations! Because you have this book in your hand, you recognize the importance and impact of face-to-face (F2F) communication. Although we now live in a 24/7 online digital world, the ability to interact and connect in person in real time is increasingly important. Why? Because being able to do so has become exceedingly rare. As more people circumvent face-to-face opportunities, those who capitalize on them will stand out from the crowd in both their professional and social lives. You get to be one of them!

Over a thousand consultants of a big four consulting firm gathered in Florida from all over the world for a global conference. In the main ballroom, they listened intently as the senior vice president described their mandate: "Stop relying on technology to communicate with clients and increase your number of face-to-face meetings with them." The attendees were cell phone–wearing, laptop-carrying, BlackBerry®-holding adults of varying ages who were hearing that they now needed to adopt an in-person component to their communication. I was there to teach them how to start, build and maintain those conversations and connections so that they could grow their businesses. Many of the attendees were uncomfortable with the prospect of the face-to-face mandate.

A survey of 4,125 MBA recruiters (Wall Street Journal, September 20, 2006) confirms two decades of research that identifies the top leadership attributes of sought-after job candidates: interpersonal and communication skills. Early in the process of writing this book's proposal, I talked to Pat, a longtime member of the FBI, who confirmed the importance of face-to-face and real-time connections: "The younger investigators are technically brilliant; they can research and ferret out the most pertinent and intricate bits of information online. They text message and are resourceful digital experts. However, we've noticed they avoid using their phones to talk to people and don't schedule meetings with potential informants. Because of that, they don't have the sources every agent needs in the field. Believe me, the people we need as sources aren't texting. It's a dilemma."

No matter how many text messages or e-mails we send and receive, online global conferences we attend, or blogs we read and write, we also need to be comfortable and confident in person. Whether it's an interview, a client presentation, a business lunch, a division meeting or a friend's wedding, we need to know how to interact, how to behave, and how to connect with others in a diverse shared social space.

Face to Face is a practical playbook that highlights situations requiring a personal touch in the face-to-face space. This book is specifically geared to address those issues that baffle, confuse, and stymie us because they're unpredictable and uncomfortable. Whether you're a senior executive, a seasoned salesperson, a career changer or career seeker, or simply a slightly shy professional, this book is for you.

Every day, newspapers contain stories that show we're at a national loss for words. The national average of those of us who self-identify as shy increased from 80 percent in 1985 to 93 percent in 2000. Dr. Philip Zimbardo, one of the founders of the Stanford Shyness Clinic, attributes this major increase to the use of technology. However, many situations that we encounter on a daily basis in both our professional and personal life require "face time"—those in-person moments where we have to communicate, whether it's with our local barista, hairstylist, boss, coworkers or employees, clients, auto mechanic, professor, or even inlaws.

Major multinational companies are recognizing the importance of personal face-to-face contact as part of business growth and building the bottom line. "Nokia CEO Plans to Make Housecalls" was an August 10, 2006, headline in the Wall Street Journal. The article led with the news that CEO Kallasvuo will spend a week per month in the United States, although he could pick up the phone instead (the CEO of Nokia has unlimited cell phone minutes, of course). "Instead of the handset, he is opting for a hands-on approach," the article continued. I would add that Kallasvuo opted for the handshake approach. The CEO is banking on face-to-face communication to regain Nokia's marketing position as is the CEO of Nissan, who is traveling around the country to meet with Nissan dealers and listen to their concerns and suggestions.

Forward-thinking industry leaders are leading us back to in-person interactions. "Formal face-to-face meetings will disappear" is the hue and cry of alleged futurists. The reality is that the opposite is true. Meeting spaces are proliferating; convention centers are expanding. Corporate giants are still going the distance to make the contacts that matter—face to face, handshake to handshake. Using technology to stay in contact in order to share facts, figures, and data makes sense. When we use technology to avoid human interaction, we may save time, but we lose out on the opportunity to build rapport, trust, and connections, as well as the unexpected benefits that happen in the face-to-face space.

"The peril of getting to know classmates on the computer is that incoming undergraduates may forget how to do so in real life." So New York University (NYU) offered an orientation seminar for incoming freshmen called Facebook in the Flesh. David Schacter, assistant dean, began, "It's face to face . . . it's social and it happens in the same space." He even had to explain how to have face-to-face interactions (New Yorker, September 17, 2007). Face to Face is the NYU seminar without the cost of college tuition.

Because companies are recognizing that creating face-to-face rapport and connection pays off, they're getting results that build their bottom line. The next wave for recruiting, hiring and promoting will be those who have the face-to-face skills as well as the required professional and technical experience.

Major university research across the country indicates that our social relationships and interactions in our personal space keep us healthy, mentally alert and contribute to our longevity. Who would argue with that? There's also a powerful personal benefit from mastering face-to-face space. According to Daniel Gilbert, Harvard professor and author of Stumbling on Happiness, "Relationships with friends and family are the #1 factor that determines our happiness."

Too many of us avoid conversations with others we meet. Whether we're standing in line at the supermarket or cleaners or waiting for the subway or for our children after their soccer practice, we often don't start impromptu conversations. It may be that we fear face-to-face rejection. But there are rewards for taking that risk in the form of new information, a new contact or a new friend.

Face to Face provides strategies for those impromptu conversations so that you can also benefit from the opportunities you encounter. My book offers solutions to the digital dilemma so that you can honey our in-person skills. As with my other books, I have combined my conversational voice with the practical "how to" and "how not to" authorial style for which I'm known.

Being facile when we're face to face is valuable, not instead of online digital communication but in concert with it. Because I have written books, articles and a blog about various areas of communication for over two decades, I've explored the new research while revisiting and reiterating prior musings that fit under the face-to-face umbrella. Points that bear repeating are repeated. Whether it's the business meal, the politics of the office, the use of our techie gizmos and gadgets or reciprocating a mentor or gathering the fruits of the grapevine, each opportunity contributes to our facility in the face-to-face space.

This book goes outside and beyond rooms to include a panoply of situations where offline face-to-face encounters occur. There are anecdotes, antidotes, suggestions, quotes, quips, and cartoons. This material, which is down to earth and back to basics, includes steps, ideas, and processes to reclaim your personal touch and help you navigate the waters of the face-to-face world.

Chapter One

Small to Medium to Big Talk

s we meet with others in the face-to-face space, many of our initial conversations begin with a getting-to-know-you exchange, or small talk. "Meeting with people in person gives us the opportunity to truly connect with them," according to psychologist Dr. Nando Pelusi (Psychology Today, November/ December 2007, p. 689). Some people sneer at small talk and dismiss it as banal or trivial and a waste of precious time. That's a huge mistake, because small talk allows us to connect with others and establish common interests. Many people avoid face-to-face time because they're neither comfortable nor confident in their abilities to communicate in person. They may be forfeiting amazing opportunities.

I asked more than a hundred successful people who I thought were great conversationalists (and I'm a tough grader), "To what skill do you most attribute your success?" Their number one answer was the ability to converse.

In these competitive, multitasking times, there are people so focused on their agendas, their quotas, their digital techie tools, their professional and personal obligations and their bottom line that they forget their spoken words contribute to the chemistry and connections with their clients, colleagues, friends, and families. Others take pride in being urgent, get-to-the-point, terse people who have more important things on their mind than small talk, which they feel is insignificant drivel. Nothing could be further from the truth. Life and work flow more smoothly when we're comfortable with conversation and, more importantly, when we know how to make others feel comfortable. We need to embrace small talk because it leads to big talk.

UNEQUIVOCAL EQUATION

In the early 1990s, Dr. Thomas Harrell, professor emeritus of business at Stanford University, studied a group of MBAs a decade after their graduation. His goal was to identify the traits of those who were most successful. He found that grade-point average had no bearing on success. However, the one common trait he identified among those who were successful was their verbal fluency. They were confident conversationalists who could talk to anyone face-to-face colleagues, investors, strangers, bosses associates. They could speak well in front of audiences, and they were easy to talk to in meetings, on airplanes, at events and casually over beverages at receptions. They started with small talk and segued through Medium Talk to Big Talk about business, interests, technology, and trends. These savvy businesspeople possessed the skills of successful leaders: the ability to converse, connect and communicate in myriad situations. The unequivocal equation is verbal fluency = success and affluency.

If we want to be successful, we need to develop and enhance our conversational prowess in the face-to-face space. Schmooze or lose is the rule for both personal and professional success. Schmooze means relaxed, friendly, easygoing conversation. Period. End of story. There is no end result that is preplanned as a goal. Formal research from Harvard to Stanford and places in between indicates that the ability to converse and communicate is a key factor of successful leaders. Oral communication skills are consistently rated in the top three most important skill sets in surveys by universities and workplace specialists.

While we're able to communicate digitally, we still must be proficient in the face-to-face shared space as well as in cyberspace. As corporations continue to merge, jobs disappear and industries are offshored, we need conversation and communication more than ever before. Networks of loyal customers and professional and personal relationships become pivotal. We not only establish, develop and nurture those relationships by our actions but also by our exchanges and our face-to-face conversations.

While we want to start with brilliant, scintillating, and/or illuminating commentary, the reality is that we start with small talk. These comments are also known as icebreakers. I prefer to call them ice melters, which slowly but surely meld and mix our conversations, questions, answers and interests as we establish common bonds.

Some of us are naturally briefer in our conversations. Saving nanoseconds by eliminating conversational connectins with people makes no sense at all in business or in personal life. By the time we leave the planet, we may have saved an hour by avoiding those moments. Big deal. If we invest in the pleasantries of small talk to establish rapport and confirm connections, we'll probably be happier, richer and have more friends.

DON'T JOIN THE DENIGRATORS

My survey of those hundred great conversationalists yielded two results one of which stunned me. The first is that 75 percent of the responders, people whom I considered to be great conversationalists, still thought of themselves as shy. I was shocked. Several admitted to working through shyness, but at times they still felt uncomfortable. They could have fooled me! In fact, they did. They worked through it so well that I found them to be exemplary at face-to-face conversation.

The second result was that not one of my great chatters denigrated small talk. They simply saw it as a way of getting to know people, putting others at ease as well as themselves, and finding common ground. Different attitude, different outcome. Not to sound Socratic, but my deduction is clear: "therefore only challenged conversationalists denigrate small talk.

Think about it. Have you ever had a wonderful conversation

with someone who had no interest in the little things that start, move, and expand verbal exchanges? I think not. Only those who aren't good at or comfortable with small talk make light of it and, in fact, put it down.

MEDIUM RARE

Medium talk is the transitional exchange that builds on small-talk topics and segues to larger issues. For example, you may start talking about the event venue, the food, and how the venue was recognized for supporting local soup kitchens. The other person's response will probably be on that subject. You would move then to medium talk, which might include how your company or you as an individual is involved in providing volunteer servers for the program.

The transition occurs when you bring your newest project or company into the conversation about a neutral topic. If your conversational companion is not adept at exchanges, you can ask about his or her projects or company policies and programs. And the conversation may organically move back to small talk and then hopscotch to BIG TALK.

SMALL TALK LEADS TO BIG TALK

In most situations, BIG TALK—murder, war, famine, pestilence, and papal edict 123—is not a verbal exchange starter. At a museum fund-raiser for students of the arts, not everyone wants to hear your views on the latest virus or border skirmish. Also, no matter how big or important current issues are, you must know the right time and place for them. You can move to bigger issues once rapport and connection are established.

Because small talk is the biggest talk we do, we need a collective attitude shift. Because it builds, develops and nurtures relationships, conversation is how we strengthen the safety net of people who make up our personal and professional networks, our

Rolodex™ (buddy lists, databases, and friends) of sources and re-sources. You could say we ought to build our rolodexterity". Small talk is valuable. It's how we find common interests/bonds and exchange information, preferences, ideas, and opinions on issues through small talk. It's how we melt the ice and get a sense of who people are—what they like and what they are like. And it doesn't always have to be about small subjects. I've often heard people getting to know one another by having casual conversations about art, economics, government programs or health issues.

Small talk is what we do to start the exchange that moves to medium talk and then builds to big talk. It's the schmoozing that cements relationships and ultimately leads to success.

"Conversations are quasi-relationships. Every second you're with someone, every word or sentence you exchange extends the relationship," said Tim Gunn, cohost of Project Runway (Wall Street Journal, "Small Talk," October 25, 2007).

THIS IS HOW WE DO IT

Information is power. Building a knowledge bank helps us start and contribute to face-to-face conversations with more ease and interest. Whether online or in print, reading a newspaper or news source each day is a must! That's how we glean conversational subject matter. Some people balk at this suggestion until they try it. This is not only the best way to invest in the knowledge bank from which to draw conversation, but it can also be fun, entertaining and informative. Whether it's online or on paper, the newspaper is full of conversation topics. If you're not a reader, lis-ten to or watch a news program or visit your favorite news blogs.

Why should a busy person with a multitude of demands on his or her time read a daily newspaper? As my fifth-grade teacher, Mrs. Kurtz, said, "A good conversationalist is well read, well versed and well rounded." He or she knows what is going on in the world and can talk about it. Reading the paper makes face-to-face conversation infinitely more manageable.

THE DESKTOP TWIST ON NEWS

Whether it's from Google, Yahoo!, AOL, or another source, we can get news bits delivered to our desktop and even our cell phone. We can visit any number of news sites, blogs or podcasts for the latest on an infinite variety of subjects. We have instant access to news locally and globally.

It makes us aware of popular culture and industry information. You do not have to be a "Dead Head" to know about the legacy of Jerry Garcia or a "Trekkie" to know about Mr. Spock and the newest Star Trek movie. Nor do you have to be a teenager to be aware of the PussyCat Dolls, the newest version of War of World Craft, or the latest trends at Comic-Con. We can talk about sports, movies, current events, and the latest famous trial, from Scopes to Scott Peterson to O.J.; there will always be a famous trial, celebrity arrest or medical discovery.

Do you have to be an expert on everything? Absolutely not. But you can be sufficiently good well read to initiate or contribute to conversations. You need enough knowledge of general topics to pose intelligent questions.

Hot Tip

We must listen to the answers to our questions and comment on them, not bring up the price of iPods or Porsches when someone is talking about Darfur or Darjeeling tea.

Intelligent questions invite others to speak about their own areas of expertise and interest. They also give us the chance to learn from what other people say. Every event, meeting or party becomes an educational opportunity that provides us with additional information and resources to provide food for thoughtful conversation.

SMALL TALKING FACE TO FACE

There are three ways to make conversation, which I call the trifecta or talking: Observe, Ask, Reveal. OAR helps us paddle through small talk safely. In my presentations, I often have my audience pair up for the small-talk attitude shift. Using the OAR™ method, they have to find something small in the room to talk about with their partner. People have picked chandeliers, crown molding, wallpaper, fire exit signs, and on two occasions shoes (my red and black heels). And in two to three minutes the conversations organically move, shift and twist to medium talk and then to big talk. The small talk never ends up where it started, and common interests are always revealed.

Small-Talk Topics

This is the easy part. Almost anything in our visual path is fair game: the venue, the food or the decor. As we face people, we can see their name badges, which provide information and bait for conversation hooks. In most areas, a comment about the traffic or finding a parking space is applicable.

Provide people with visual small-talk topics: a tie, a pin, a scarf. To underscore this point, we should give people a visual hook. And when we see that invitation to comment, we can respond with the bait for further conversation.

Some Possible Openers

- "The food looks great."
- "I see by your tie that you're a golfer."
- "I'm so glad I made it on time. The traffic was incredible."
- "Have you been to this hotel before for an event?
- "Would you recommend I join this association even though I'm new to the industry?"
- "Whoa! The (heat, rain, snow, fog) caused so much traffic. I was almost late."

SULTANS OF SEGUE

How do you move on to the next topic of conversation? the sultans of segue move with a subtle flow that continues the seamless process of the face-to-face exchange. There are magic phrases, responses and general comments that create bridges and start building the big conversation. Some of them are also handy for sidestepping or diffusing difficult people, as well as for politely moving the interchange along.

- "I hadn't thought of it that way. How did you come to that?"
- "That's a new way of looking at it."
- "It reminds me of . . ."

BORROW OTHER PEOPLE'S LIVES

On a daily basis, most of us get to hear others' interesting, amusing or thoughtful stories that make a point. If you hear a story of interest to you, it will most likely be interesting to others as well.

I don't have children, so I borrow my friends' stories. I also borrow the stories of my Xtreme athlete friends, skilled crafts people, gardening experts and excellent cooks, since these are things I don't do—let alone do well. Becky Gordon's quilts connect me to quilters, and Marcie's gardening connects me to those who plant, prune and grow. The stories of all my friends' children connect me to the parents I meet in business or social situations. When the parents in my circle share their stories in exasperation, I often hear the humor, which is defined in the Talmud as tragedy + time. Borrowing other people's lives helps us relate to those we meet with whom we may not easily see a similarity.

The brothers Heath (Chip and Dan) demonstrate how we remember stories in their brilliant book, Made to Stick (Random House, New York, January 2007, p. 243). During an exercise of one-minute speeches, the students "are unable to remember a single concept." The typical Stanford student uses 2.5 statistics, and one student in ten tells a story. Sixty-three percent of the class remember the stories, but only five percent remember the statistic. "We need to tell stories that connect, confirm, inform or amuse in order to be memorable and stick in people's minds."

THE SURPRISE PARTY—KAREN'S STORY

When I was speaking in Dallas, Karen Cortell Reisman and I met for a beverage, and she shared a story after I asked about her son and daughter. I cracked up because it gave a whole new digital meaning to the term surprise party.

"No kidding! It really was a surprise party with a twist," shared Karen. "We took our son and five of his friends out to a Dallas steakhouse to celebrate my son's high school graduation. The boys were delightful, had a good time and were perfect gentlemen. After dinner, I suggested they come back to our house. The twenty-minute drive home was so quiet—six boys in the car and not a sound. I just figured it was a guy thing that they didn't talk.

"We drove up to our home and there were fifty kids outside waiting for us! The boys weren't being quiet; they were quietly texting their buddy lists about coming to our house. It truly was a surprise party; however, my husband Jimmy and I were the ones who were surprised!"

Because I keep a small spiral notebook with me for such conversation fodder, I whipped out a pen and wrote this story down. Even the most unforgettable (or so we think) comment or story can get lost if we don't take time to record it somewhere. Some people use the recording memo on their cell phone. Others jot notes on their PDA. Whatever works for you. To write this book, I had to decipher spiral notebooks full of stories. The miracle: I could read them!

People say great things and tell us stories that we can quote as we "borrow" their lives, and that contributes to our conversations. "Personal history is best told and transmitted through stories, whether it's the story of our life or what just happened on the street on the way to meet someone. Your story becomes mine as you share it with me," according to Craig Harrison, a professional speaker and storyteller.

BE OF GOOD HUMOR

Humor has a special way of bringing people together, either in a small-talk conversation face to face or on the phone. It can establish rapport and warmth. Humor is a unique and magical elixir that can even heal the body.

Both management and medical research support the value of humor. Laughter is good for your health. "Laughter works by stimulating the brain to produce hormones that help ease pain. It also stimulates the endocrine system, which may relieve symptoms of disease. Laughter can also help feelings of depression," according to Dr. William Fry of Stanford Medical School. Since Dr. Fry's original research, we have read volumes of research about humor as a tonic.

You don't have to be a stand-up comic to use humor effectively. Humor can be defined in two ways. First, it's the quality of being funny. Second, it's the ability to perceive, enjoy, or express something funny. We love the person who gets our good lines and laughs.

The right sentence or phrase at the right moment can save a negotiation or a board meeting. But humor should be used judiciously, because it can offend as well as delight. I'm usually wary when I hear the phrase, "Did you hear the one about . . . ?" Often we just did, or we recently read it in a forwarded e-mail.

Humor Do's and Don'ts

Do:

- Practice your stories and punch lines. I once practiced my opening story for a presentation seventeen times. Timing is everything!

- Watch comedies, both on television and at the movies, and read books about humor. I watch Two and a Half Men, Monk, and Jon Stewart/Stephen Colbert (and way too many other comedies) with a paper and pencil by my side (and always attribute the funny lines).
- Use the AT&T rule to check any story or joke: Is it Appropriate? Is it Tasteful? Is it Timely?
- Laugh at yourself: it's a trait of people who take risks. Some of the best stories are those you tell on yourself.
- Observe for irony. One day I saw a fellow in the yoga lotus position outside Mollie Stone's supermarket. His eyes were closed in a meditative state. And, he was smoking a cigarette! Go figure! Meditative or menthol? Talk about ironic.

Don't:

- "Don't tell jokes if you don't tell them well," advised David Glickman, stand-up comic, humorist, and professional speaker.
- Don't put people down. Roasting can create a slow burn—one that can backfire.
- Don't use humor that is racist, sexist, homophobic, or that slurs religion, ethnic origin, or disability.
- Don't be afraid to let go and laugh. It's good for your health and makes working the room a lot more enjoyable.

We need to ask permission to use the stories that we hear. "That's so funny/poignant/interesting. Do you mind if I write that down?" Some people have told me that they don't mind, but they have asked me not to use their name. That's fine.

Something else happens when we respond to a story or comment and write it down. It shows we're listening, comprehending and valuing the comments. That makes a good impression.

LISTEN ACTIVELY, NOT PASSIVELY

As a raconteur and veteran small talker, I have always been sensitive to the criticism about talkers. But research shows that just because a person is a good small talker doesn't mean he or she isn't also a good listener.

All of us need to be good listeners. It helps us move to medium talk and on to big talk. It means more than staring into someone's eyes while he or she talks, while you plan tomorrow's meeting, play a John Legend tune in your head or review the movie you saw last night. Active listening means hearing what people say, concentrating on them and their words and then responding. There's a benefit to really listening and being in the moment. We improve our chances of remembering both the person and the conversation, according to Dr. Ralph Nichols's breakthrough research on listening skills.

In some of my presentations, people practice role-playing as talkers and listeners. Thousands of talkers have said that the most important behaviors of active listening—the things that most encouraged them to talk—were what I call the Magnificent Seven of Listening.

Magnificent Seven of Listening

1. Making eye contact (We can't make eye contact if we're scanning a room or checking our e-mail, text messages, or the television show we downloaded on our cell phone.)
2. Nodding
3. Smiling and/or laughing
4. Asking relevant questions that indicate interest
5. Making statements that reflect similar situations
6. Using body language that is open and receptive
7. Bringing the conversation full circle

Robert Levy, Esq., attributes his success to his interest, ability, and willingness to listen. He is executive director of the New Jersey Association of Mortgage Bankers and, at twenty-nine years of age, was the youngest deputy commissioner of banking in New Jersey. "I was surrounded by industry people with more experience and skills than I had. I became an observer and listener and learned from their stories about their mistakes, so I avoided making the same errors. I didn't want to be the person unaware of history, who was doomed to repeat it. Listening and respecting my experienced colleagues was an education that has served me well." We can all learn from Levy's advice on listening to those who are experienced and save ourselves from making unnecessary mistakes.

Five Fundamental Laws of Scintillating Small Talk

1. Be a conversational chameleon. Adapt conversation to the individual by age, interest, profession and geographic region. We talk to five-year-olds differently that we talk to ten-year-olds or thirty-year-olds.
2. Be a name dropper. Always mention the names of people, places, or organizations that you might have in common with someone. In this six-degree-of-separation small world, you never know!
3. Borrow other people's lives. Share the stories of your friends who have kids or Web sites, study tae kwon do, are Xtreme athletes, or have opera tickets, even if you don't. It helps connect us to people with different interests.
4. Be a two-timer. Give people a second chance. They may have been distracted the first time you met.
5. Be nice to everyone. Don't judge tomorrow's book by today's cover.

Allow me to expand on the last point. Being nice to everyone includes the service professionals we encounter on a daily basis, whether it's the checkout person at the supermarket, the counter person at the dry cleaners or the server at your local coffee shop.

Whether it's a kind word, a "how are you," or a comment about the weather, which is indeed very small talk, it's significant to the people who stand on their feet for eight hours a day providing a service.

Four Fatal Flaws of Casual Conversation

1. Being unprepared. Not having your self-introduction in mind
2. Not reading papers, Web sites or information sources as fodder for conversation
3. Killing conversations by:
   - Asking a barrage of questions, no matter how open-ended, and not listening to the answers. "Interrogations" are no substitute for conversations.
   - Complaining (kvetching). It sets a negative tone for small talk.
   - Monopolizing and manipulating. This doesn't open the door for the shy person who has a lot to offer.
   - One-upping/competing, which is a way of putting others down and closes the door.
   - Using off-color language.
   - Interrupting, which is a universal irritant.
   - Correcting. It's an insult, especially when done in front of others.
   - Scanning the room.
4. Not listening (Keep MP3 Earbuds out of ears, Bluetooth® off ears, BlackBerrys® out of sight.)

If we're conscious of listening actively, our small talk organically segues to a more meaningful, deeper exchange. Face-to-face conversation has been said to be a dying art, but with preparation and a positive attitude about small talk, we can revive it!

ROANE'S REMINDERS

* Adjust your attitude about small talk to be the grand opener for big talk.
* Read one newspaper a day, either online or on paper. Local, national, and international conversation starters fill the pages.
* Clip and collect cartoons, announcements, of interest to you and your network. Or send a hyperlink with an e-mail note.
* Read newszines, professional journals, minutes and blogs for up-to-the-minute topics of conversation.
* Take note and take notes when you hear something interesting or observe the odd or absurd.
* Use humor (surely you jest!) carefully. Be lighthearted and don't take yourself too seriously. No dissing of others.
* Listen actively with ears, eyes and heart. Truly pay attention. Ditch the techie gadgets.
* Just say yes to new opportunities. Doing, seeing, visiting something new and beyond our everyday interests gives us something to talk about

Chapter Two

How to Shine in a Crowd

t's important that we comfortably and confidently interact with people live and in person. There are myriad times when the venue is the face-to-face space, and we're expected to show up and bring our personal touch to the experience.

It may be an industry party following your company's new product launch, an industry convention, a trade show, a fundraiser or your neighbor's wedding. It's a huge room full of people, several hundred of them—many of whom you don't know. And you have to attend. You need to mix, mingle, meet people, and be sociable in this face-to-face space. It can be daunting. Where do you start? What do you say? What do you do?

This chapter is about how to shine in any crowd and how to turn a daunting experience into an opportunity for business and social success—and have fun in the process. I've included many ideas, suggestions and tips that will serve you in the workplace as well as in social situations.

WHO ARE THESE PEOPLE?

We have more in common with people than we may know. Whether they're of different backgrounds, ages or professions, perhaps 90 percent of the people we meet at business or social events work hard, have families and hobbies, and enjoy (or suffer) the same weather, economy, vacation destinations and computer glitches that we do. They have favorite sports teams, hobbies, restaurants, music and books. Whether their title is boss, board member, client, colleague, coworker, neighbor or friend, they have full lives that include families, friends and interests.

Most of us were raised to be thoughtful, kind and well mannered, even though some of us may not mind all our manners all the time. We want to connect with our peers, friends and colleagues, have good conversations and have a good time in our offline face-to-face world. According to Om Malik, who runs technology blog GigaOM, "Human beings have an overwhelming need to get together, communicate and interact. Our genes are coded that way" (Business 2.0, May 2007, p. 52).

ZITS   **BY JERRY SCOTT AND JIM BORGMAN**

Zits King.

ZITS@ZITS Partnership, King Features Syndicate.

So, the first thing to remember as we face a crowd of people is that other attendees want to talk to us, too. They are just as eager as we are to make connections, to be relaxed, and to talk, share, and get to know others and hang out. Nobody shows up to stand alone in that shared space and feel conspicuous, uncomfortable and dorky.

Showing up, although a good start, is not enough; it is only how we open the door. If we don't step into the room, we miss out on all the opportunities, possibilities, and serendipity that happen in the face-to-face (F2F) space.

A GREAT, NOT GRAND, ENTRANCE

Whether entering an industry or social cocktail party for hundreds, a conference hall, a ballroom or a ballgame, stop and take a deep breath. Survey the setting so that you get the lay of the land (and land mines). Where are the bars? The buffet? The groups? The people standing alone? Get a feel for the energy in the room and for how people are behaving. Walk in with your head held high, and head for the host, the greeter or people you recognize (provided you don't stay with them throughout the event).

Still have butterflies in your stomach? That makes you normal! To successfully schmooze in a crowd, we need to prepare ourselves to feel confident and practice the strategies that contribute to our comfort and conversational success. What keeps us from being at ease with meeting and mingling? I've identified the specific roadblocks and some remedies we can use to overcome them.

Hot Tip

Follow the lead of shy people, who come to an event within fifteen minutes of the start time. That way, they're not walking into crowded rooms of people already clustered in groups.

The Strangers in the Night—or Day—Pitfall

When we were growing up, our parents may have told us, "Don't talk to strangers." Some of us are still unconsciously following that advice, even though it's not very useful as we manage or change our careers, grow our businesses or enjoy our lives! If we avoid strangers at our professional association luncheon, an alumni event, a wedding, a Chamber of Commerce mixer, or a client-sponsored soiree, we'll not only have a terrible time, we'll miss opportunities!

Remedy: Redefine the term stranger. Before you go anywhere,

think about what you have in common with the people attending the event. To gather more information, you can Google the event, the organization, or the venue. Once you've established a common thread with people, topics for conversation become obvious. That leads to confidence, which attracts people. And the cycle goes on.

The Proper Introduction Pitfall

Because many of us were taught to speak only to people to whom we've been properly introduced, we wait for someone else to do the work of introducing us, preferably with enthusiasm and energy. The bad news is it ain't gonna happen! We're on our own.

Remedy: Have a planned, practiced self-introduction.

Self-Introduction Tips

1. Your introduction should be seven to nine seconds in length. (The thirty-second or longer self-promotional elevator pitch is not appropriate.)

2. Lean into the introduction. Extending yourself is a trait of great hosts. Just be mindful that many people need twelve to eighteen inches of personal space, so don't go inside that. Unlike the classic Seinfeld episode of "The Close Talker," we shouldn't invade others' personal space.

3. Accompany your introduction with a smile and firm web-to-web handshake. Avoid the finger squeeze and the jellyfish hand.

4. Give the benefit of what you do rather than name, rank and serial number.

5. Match your self-introduction to each situation to give others a context for your presence.

Example: "Hi, I'm Jeff Jones, and I help people sleep at night. Nice to meet you." Jeff has given a benefit that allows the other person to ask him what he does. "Oh, I am a financial planner." Then

Jeff stops talking about himself and says these magic words: "And what about you?" Now there is an exchange and duo-logue.

Deliver your introduction with energy, enthusiasm, and appropriate animation—but remember: This book isn't Attila's Guerilla Guide to Shark-Infested Negotiation. It's about managing and excelling in real space—face to face. I leave the strategies for maneuvering, mangling, manipulating, and overworking the room to others.

You Never Know!

Always go to an event with a focus, not an agenda. When we behave as though we have an agenda, it's often off-putting. Be open to serendipity—those unexpected good things that happen while we're planning something else! The theme of my book How to Create Your Own Luck was based on these unplanned, you-never-know, six-degrees-or-less, small-world experiences we have when we show up in the face-to-face space.

When Bill Farley was the vice president of marketing for Playboy Enterprises, his wife Judy often accompanied him to events at The Mansion (yes, that Mansion!). She saw a fellow standing alone who had won a contest to be a guest at a Playboy event. "I went over to chat with him to make him feel at ease. I asked where he was from, and when he said Palm Beach, it struck a chord. I mentioned that a best friend of mine from my teaching days in Chicago lived there, but we had lost contact. When he asked her name, I told him. He looked at me and said, 'She's one of my best clients. I even have her phone number programmed on my cell phone. Would you like to talk to her?'" Judy Farley was nearly speechless, but she said yes. Seconds later, she was reconnected with a long-lost friend because of a small-world face-to-face experience. Because Judy was helping Bill welcome guests, her reward was a rekindled friendship. You never know!

The Waiting for Godot Pitfall

"Good things come to those who wait" is outdated, inaccurate thinking. Remember that if we wait for people to approach us, the wait is interminably long.

Remedy: When it comes to meeting and mingling, the RoAne version applies: "Good things come to those who initiate."

Judy Farley regained a friend because she tried to make a stranger feel comfortable. We don't have to know everything, or even a lot, about a subject in order to make conversation about it. We just need to be interested in others and well read or well versed enough to ask good questions, listen to the answers, and respond appropriately.

THE MAGIC FORMULA: ACT LIKE A HOST

I always share Dr. Adele Scheele's timeless advice for those at face-to-face events. She suggests that successful socializers don't wait around behaving like guests. Instead, they take their innate gracious attitude to every event and act like they're the host! It's easy enough to do.

Good Hosts . . .

- Are interested in other people's comfort
- Go out of their way to mix, mingle, and connect people
- Greet others and make them feel welcome
- Introduce people to people, share stories and ask questions
- Listen to the responses
- Excuse themselves cheerfully and politely once the new kid is settled into a conversation, and move on

People tell me, "I never thought I could or should take charge like that, but when I consider it my job to meet people, put them at ease, keep the conversation flowing, and introduce them to one another, I'm actually more relaxed myself." Bingo!

There are two parts to interacting in face-to-face situations: being interesting and being interested. Acting like the host reminds us to do both. If we're interested in others, we create a memorable impression. That means people are left with more than our business card when the event is over. They remember who we are because we made them feel included and comfortable.

> **Hot Tip**
>
> If you really are the host or host organization, be sure to act like it! If it's a big event, organize an ad hoc greeting committee to help you.

When Jennifer and Sander Walker were married, I was asked to be the official greeter at the reception because they were staying at the church for an hour to take formal photos. It was an honor for me, so I made sure that each guest was greeted as well as shown the bar and the gift table. I even brought tape to make sure all cards were attached to the gifts. You could say I was their warm-up-the-guests act. It's a great idea to have a greeter at a wedding; it's a way to favor and include a special friend as part of the wedding team. The bonus for me: I got to meet everyone.

PREPARATION POLICY: THE HIGH FIVE

It's easier to shine in a crowd when we feel confident, and we feel confident when we're prepared. Here are some areas preparation for consideration before entering the face-to-face space:

1. Attitude. Savvy socializers say they look forward to events. They like people and find them interesting.

Jolie Pollard, a talent agent and event planner, shifted her attitude. "When we began our business, it was a new concept for us to enter a room full of people we had never met, introduce ourselves and our business. We were quite nervous the first time out but met some very interesting people and realized we were enjoying ourselves! The next time we had the opportunity to attend this kind of function, we looked at each other before walking into the room and said, 'I wonder who we'll get to meet today.' We do so with an air of anticipation rather than anxiety. We've never been disappointed because we always meet terrific people."

2. Focus. Know your purpose for attending, whether it's to gain visibility, be sociable, make contacts, or create goodwill or good public relations. (Caveat: We must be guided by our goals, not blinded by them!)

3. Cards. Have enough, have them accessible, and make sure they're easily read. While there are different customs in other parts of the world, in the United States we use them to follow up conversation, not to precede or replace it. Have cards with you at social and business events. They facilitate follow-up.

4. Conversation. Come to the event prepared with three open-ended questions and three stories or topics of interest that you can share.

5. A smile. Accompany your smile with eye contact, which is the key indication that you're open, approachable, and in the moment with your conversation partners.

Hot Tip

To make yourself more comfortable in a crowd, dress for the occasion. Wearing a sports jacket to a black-tie-optional event or a cocktail dress to a business occasion makes us look as if we missed the memo on attire. One way to find out the preferred dress code is to check Web sites or just pick up the phone call and ask!

NEVER UNDERESTIMATE APPROACHABILITY

Being approachable means having a pleasant countenance, visual connection, and welcoming stance. No one ever says, "Oh, look—there's a glowering, glaring sourpuss who I must meet!"

To be approachable, we must also be appropriate. Some authors and speakers advise us to be outrageous, to dress outrageously, and to say outrageous things in order to be memorable. But being memorable for the wrong reasons can backfire—for example, if we're remembered for a mean-spirited or inappropriate comment, or clothing or behavior that made people uncomfortable. Be sensible and remember to use good judgement.

THE NOSH AND NIBBLE NETWORK HOUR

Often, when there's food at an event, we tend to eat it without thinking. Eating and mingling require balance, literally and figuratively, and we have to keep our wits about us.

It's never a good idea to converse with a mouth full of food or to pile a plate so full that others notice. It's also difficult to juggle food, beverage and business cards. A business manager at my presentation in Hawaii shared his strategy, "If it's a business event, the best way to win the balancing act is to eat first (following up with a moist towelette) or even before arriving at the event." When we eat first, we can then focus and circulate.

As for the Food Question

One of my favorite quotes comes from one of the most glamorous women around, Miss Piggy: "Never eat more than you can lift."

Liquid Assets?

Let me put the drink debate to rest. At a business or quasi-business social event, we want to be sure our behavior is an asset.

When it comes to liquid refreshments, be conservative. As we face people, we want to be sure that what we do and say allows us to create rapport and that the next day, we can remember clearly the events of the prior day.

What can nondrinkers do in companies that have a hard-charging and hard-drinking culture? Some stick to club soda and continue to converse. Others hold a drink but don't drink it. Some people I interviewed said that being a nondrinker was not a problem. Others said that although they themselves were comfortable with nondrinkers, some of their drinking colleagues were not! If you don't drink, have a few comments ready in the instance that someone says something. One easy out is to say you're the designated driver or, with a smile, the designated nondrinker. Then move on to another topic.

NAME TAG TIPS

Always, always wear your name tag on the right-hand side. Although men's pockets are on the left side and it's easier to clip the name tag there, put it on the right side. It will be in the other person's line of sight as you both extend your right arms for a handshake. If the name tag is one you fill out yourself, use a thick marker so that it can be seen. Write something to pique people's curiosity—perhaps something that suggests a benefit to them.

- A massage therapist wrote "Painkiller." That was provocative and gave others a hook for questions.
- A doctor of good humor wrote "Medicine Man."

Name tags are conversation starters. If you're hosting a traditional conference where name tags are preprinted from a computer database, make sure the program prints the names Large type. If the company, title, and city are included on the name tag, people can use the information to start a conversation. "Oh, I see you're from Indianapolis. Is that city as nice as I've heard?"

One colleague suggested that at both business and social events "Where are you from originally?" is a good opener. In San Francisco, where natives are not abundant, this starts the volley. And if someone is actually from San Francisco, it's an even better conversation starter.

Joan Eisenstodt, meeting planner extraordinaire, warns against wearing hanging lanyards with name tags attached. They almost always hang in a place where you may not want people to look to catch your name!

In this technologically advanced world, some name tags can be zapped into a PDA to be added to a database. Just be sure you have a real-time exchange to ensure you make a face-to-face personal connection.

THE NAME GAME: I FORGOT!

People don't always remember names. According to Dr. Anneliese Batius, a psychiatrist at Harvard Medical School, "Forgetting is part of the normal memory system." Memory lapses are natural. Dr. Lori Samps, a psychology professor at the University of Colorado, found that the brain is more likely to link to livelihoods than names. Associate the person's face with his or her occupation and name as a way of firing up the name recall brain (Psychology Today, March/April 2005).

What should we do if we forget a name? First of all, know that we all forget names way more often than we'd like to admit.

Tell the truth. Don't waste your time trying to remember how you were supposed to remember this person's name, by putting a "cat in a hat on a vat." Instead, simply say, "It's been one of those days. I remember you, but please help me out and tell me your name." Say it lightly and slightly apologetically. People understand. It's happened to them!

Stick your hand out and say your name. People respond in kind 95 percent of the time. Believe me, if you forgot their name, they've probably forgotten yours. By saying your name, you alleviate their discomfort and give them a chance to reveal their name.

Lana Teplick said that she walked into a Subway. My immediate comment was, "I didn't know you went to New York!" She quickly corrected me, saying that it was a sandwich shop. In the shop she saw the husband of one of the surgeons she knew from the University of Southern Alabama Hospital.

"I went over and said, 'Hi, Harvey. It's Lana Teplick.'

" 'Hi. Nice to see you,' he responded.

"What he said next was telling: 'Thank you so much for saying your name. Seeing you out of context, I wouldn't have been sure who you were.' Then he added, 'Some of us get older and we get fatter, but you look terrific!'

"Because I said hello and didn't make him struggle to place my name and face, I got a great compliment."

There's no point to the cruel game of putting someone on the spot about your name. This is not how to start an engaging conversation. Successful communicators build bridges during face-to-face encounters; they don't burn them!

Make an effort to remember people's names. Read their name tag or repeat the name if you're introduced. Think about the person and look at him as you say his name. Focus on that person, not on your next conversational tidbit. Do what you can to remember, but be forgiving if you or he forgets.

Mingling mavens are civil people. We let others save face and cut people some slack. At a San Francisco Chamber of Commerce mixer, I was introduced to a woman and said, "Nice to meet you." Her response, with ice in her voice, was, "We already met." Oops! Gulp! I didn't remember her, but she felt she won the game of "Gotcha!" A better, more gracious response would have been, "Nice to see you again. I'm Carmen San Diego." I will never forget her comment and how it made me feel.

When people remember our name, the effect is memorable. My mother always remembered with great affection her second visit to New York's Latin Quarter nightclub and its owner, Lou

Walters (Barbara's father). "When the paper association had a convention in New York, several couples went to dinner at the Latin Quarter. Dad and I enjoyed the show, the food, and that Lou Walters stopped at our table and chatted with us. The next night we decided to go back, just the two of us. I will never forget that Lou Walters came over to our table, warmly greeted us by our name, and welcomed us back. With all the people he meets, he remembered us."

My mother recalled that event at a time when her memory was beginning to falter. To hear her recall each detail and the feelings Mr. Walters evoked was lovely. The reality is that Mr. Walters may have been tipped off by the host, who may have been tipped off by either of my parents saying they had such a good time that they returned. Or not. But the impact of Lou Walters's welcome lasted over four decades.

That's what good restaurant and club hosts do. We can do the same: warmly greeting people and making them feel welcomed and included, whether in our home, our office, or in a crowd at a conference.

AN INTRO TO INTROS

Traditionally, we introduce the "less important" person to the "more important" person. We know that everyone is important, but these are arbitrary societal conventions. "Mr. Cummins, I'd like you to meet Patrick Skov. Patrick, this is Sherwood Cummins, the founder of Recreate."

We introduce peers by name and give a bit of information they can use to carry on the conversation. "Michael, have you met Jennifer Walker, our super PR person? Jennifer, this is Michael Berringer, who's with the hospital's computer training department."

Letitia Baldrige makes introductions very simple in her book The New Complete Guide to Executive Manners (Maxwell Macmillan, New York, 1993). She says that the most important thing to remember about introducing people is to do it, "even if you forget names, get confused or blank out on the proper procedure."

Ms. Baldrige's Guidelines for Introductions

"Introducing people is one of the most important acts in business life."

1. Introduce a younger person to an older person.
2. Introduce a peer in your own company to a peer in another company.
3. Introduce a nonofficial to an official person.
4. Introduce a junior executive to a senior executive.
5. Introduce a fellow executive to a customer or client.

THE "WHO'S WHO?"

I am often asked, "How do we approach people in positions of power?" With manners, respect and appropriate etiquette. Use titles (Doctor, Senator, Mayor, Reverend, Duke, Rabbi, Your Honor, Admiral, General, Detective, Mr. or Ms.). Include last names. Only move to a first name when invited to do so. When I spoke to my client in the Air Force, I always addressed him as Captain Bell (now Major Bell), never as Aaron, on the phone, in e-mail, and in person, although he's younger than I am.

Don't presume familiarity. Is this old-fashioned? Perhaps, but what's the risk? That someone will accuse us of having good old-fashioned manners? We should live so long! The alternative is to risk being memorable for mangled manners!

Hot Tip

Avoid nicknaming people who you've just met. When introduced to Robert, don't address him as Bob, unless invited to do so.

I have never introduced myself as anything but Susan and am amazed (read annoyed) at people who call me Sue. What to do? If the nickname bothers you, pleasantly correct the person and say (with a smile in your voice and on your face), "By the way, it's Susan" (or Joseph, Judith, Samuel, Gabriella).

When you do get to meet the CFO of the company, the mayor or George Clooney (dreaming right along), your icebreaker opening comment should be focused on that person:

- "It's a pleasure to meet you, (Mayor)."
- "Your work on the restructuring was so impressive, (CFO)."
- "Good Night and Good Luck was one of my favorite films, (Mr. Clooney)," or, "Your work on behalf of Darfur is inspiring, (Mr. Clooney)."
- "People magazine got it right: you are the sexiest, (Mr. Clooney)!" (As you can tell, George Clooney is my favorite actor.)

If you have a request or issue to discuss, ask the VIP if there's a preferred way to contact his or her office. That way, this person can give you the name of an assistant or may even give you a business card.

Hot Tip
Be sure to follow up within two days!

BREAKING AND ENTERING

So many of us get to a mixer, party, or meeting and find people are already gathered in groups, having conversations and enjoying themselves. What should we do? Leave? Certainly not!

If you've just walked into a gathering in progress, first introduce yourself to the host or greeter. Then scan the room and look for the most animated group of three to five people. It's tougher to go over to two people, since they could be engaged in an intimate or otherwise important conversation. With two people, we might be interrupting; with three or more, we're joining.

Joining a group can be so uncomfortable. Pick a lively, upbeat group, and stand on the periphery with open, agreeable body language. Make sounds like "hm" or "mmm," nod, and smile. When someone invites you by words, eye contact, or facial expression to step into the group, introduce yourself and say something pleasant. Don't be afraid you'll have nothing to contribute. It's highly unlikely that these people will be discussing quantum physics or other subjects about which you may know nothing.

I learned another way to join a group from a charming Canadian woman who attended one of my presentations. She informed us that she used a different approach when people were already in groups. She stood near an animated group of three or four people. When someone looked her way and there was a break in conversation, she asked, "Do you mind if I join you?" She had an upbeat, pleasant voice and tone. And a big smile. "No one has ever said, 'Yes, we mind!' People always stepped back to include me."

Warning: This is not the time for a thirty-second self-promotional pitch or even a fifteen-second one! You're an invited guest in this conversation, not the star. Believe it or not, there are some people in my audiences who have asked me how to get into groups and change small-talk conversations to business. And it's always about their business, their agenda. My answer is always, "Don't." Other people do not live to fulfill our agenda.

YENTA, THE MATCHMAKER

The best socializers are the conversationalists who bring others into the group with enough information, enthusiasm, and respect to make the group want to include the new kid on the block. Even when she has just met the new person, Yenta remembers most of what was said and adds that into the mix.

Lukewarm Introduction: "Jane, meet Joe."

Yenta's Introduction: "Jane is our accountant and a marathon runner. Joe is our union representative. He has a fascinating hobby: he windsurfs all over the world."

Introductions should create a warm reception and "make a match."

Lest you think that wind surfing or surfing the waves hasn't impacted business careers, it can be the very reason for the new job offer (Fast Company, November 2007, pp. 8–9). Mike Brown was an avid surfer who worked for the City of Irvine as an environmental manager. Yvon Chouinard, the founder of Patagonia, was also an avid surfer. Both of them used Greg Liobie, the same surfboard maker, who thought they ought to meet. They did. Their meeting turned into an informal job interview after which they went surfing. Mike Brown became Patagonia's vice president of sustainability, the first in the country. "We went from the surfboard to the turf board because of an astute acquaintance."

Matchmakers are making a comeback in their original field of interest featured in the classic play Fiddler on the Roof. Yes, people are hiring traditional matchmakers, their personal yentas, who will personally find what online searches at Match.com and other sites failed to produce: the perfect love match. Featured on the Today Show and in a New York Times article (September 30, 2007), these referrals take place after a face-to-face meeting, which gives the matchmaker a much better sense of who might be the perfect match. Much like headhunters for the career-minded, traditional matchmakers are in the business of using their personal touch to make the right introductions.

I myself played matchmaker for my college roommate. Introductions made with the right information can make a difference and a match. The good news: although they divorced after thirty years, she still talks to me!

SHINING THE LIGHT IN A CROWD

Those who shine in a crowd have another universal trait: they shine the light on others in the crowd because they are inclusive, engaging and nonjudgmental.

Patricia Fripp is one of the best at doing this. Although she's a well-known national public speaker and executive speech coach who is often recognized, she always shines the light on others. She starts off by sharing an enthusiastic comment or two about the new person and then eases that person into the group conversation. Patricia acts like the host. She includes people with eye contact, words, body language, and her welcoming presence.

When you extend yourself to someone and invite her into your group conversation, you become memorable. People remember and refer business to someone who has included them.

ROUND-TABLE TALK

There you are at the Chamber of Commerce, conference board, job fair or professional association luncheon or dinner, or offline beer blast of your online list serve, seated at a round table with several other attendees. No more moving around for a while. You're stuck where you are and have only limited choices of people with whom to make conversation. Sometimes it's a bonus to be stuck with someone; other times it's not. In either case, make the most of it. Engage the people on either side of you with pleasantries and small talk. There's another option:

Hot Tip

Be the table host. Ask everyone to go around the table and give a ten-second introduction. Carl LaMell, president of Clearbrook, says, "People are very appreciative for the opportunity to meet everyone at the table. Then they all have the choice of talking to people seated on either side or across the table."

PARTING IS SUCH SWEET SORROW

Extricating and exiting from a conversation (and every aspect of life) can be excruciating. Unlike our online communication, which has no tone, no body language, and no facial feedback, in the face-to-face space we can observe body language and nonverbal signals—fidgeting, glancing around the room, shifting feet, wandering attention. In other words, we can tell when our partner is ready to exit. We're memorable if we notice the signals and facilitate the ending. Here are three ways to do so:

1. Friendly recap of what you discussed that emphasizes your connection: "It's been fun talking to a kindred spirit who enjoys watching the Daily Show as much as I do."
2. Get me outta here. If the exchange was not particularly fun, lively, or interesting, we can excuse ourselves and say with an upbeat tone, "I hope you enjoy the rest of the event (party, conference, ballet, picnic, etc.)!"
3. A great get away. Diane Parente, president of Image Development and Management, Inc., has the most charming and gracious exit. She focuses on others, listens and responds accordingly. She always has a smile on her face and puts others at ease. Diane observes her conversational partners for cues, and when it's time to move on, she says, "I shouldn't monopolize your time. I know you want to meet other people. I've really enjoyed talking with you about ____ (you fill in the blank)."

Instead of leaning into our exiting remarks, we move slightly back. The conversation is summarized or an exchange acknowledged. The next step is to move about one-quarter of the room away to someone else or another group.

Remember: If the person wasn't particularly warm or receptive, it may have had nothing to do with you. He may have just learned that his child did poorly on SATs, that his mother has fallen and broken her hip, or that his company may be downsizing. Or he just might be coming down with the flu. You never know. Regardless of how your exchange went, be polite.

Another way to exit is the "come on along" approach used by the late Dr. Irving Siegel, founding fellow of the American College of Obstetricians and Gynecologists. At conferences he acted like a host and would often say to a young doctor, "Dr. Wojtal, I see Dr. Wara. Why don't you join me and I'll introduce you?"

Rather than leave the person, Dr. Siegel introduced her to colleagues and helped Dr. Wojtal increase her comfort, contacts, and collegial circle. That's memorable—and each of us can do it!

MEDICAL MINGLING REMINDERS

Remember that some people need you to speak more loudly and more clearly. And some may have early arthritis or carpal tunnel syndrome, so don't squeeze or shake hands too hard.

If you have a specific problem, just say, "I'd love to shake your hand, but I just sprained my thumb." That gives the person information and an explanation. Otherwise, you might be perceived as rude and standoffish. This is another case where the truth can start a conversation. You've disclosed something about yourself and given information that could prompt questions or comments. And that's what we want to do—share something that will spark interest, encourage questions, and start conversation.

> **Hot Tip**
> In this global, diverse world, we'll meet people of varying abilities. If you see someone cupping his ear, the ambient noise is a problem. Be sure to face this person as you speak clearly.

SPOUSAL SUPPORT: YOURS AND THEIRS

Our associates' spouses, significant others and guests have a great deal of influence, so we must include them and be gracious to them. I've been to several events and met siblings, friends and parents who were guests. Not being gracious or inclusive can create a bad impression that will last.

Many spouses at job-related events are now male, but the majority are still women who are intelligent and involved in their own careers and/or in the community. We all share experiences of the weather, community issues (traffic, parking, road repairs, school bonds and programs, literacy and library issues), political events, and cultural events that are easy to discuss with others' spouses.

How we talk to our own spouses/significant others in public is equally important. I've heard comments about people who made others uncomfortable by being less than gracious to their own spouses. Showing your spouse respect and civility raises both her and you in people's eyes.

CORRECTION FLUID, FLUID CORRECTIONS

It's as much how we say things as what we say. At certain times, we may need to correct people who have made inaccurate or misleading comments, but there's a right time, place and manner for these corrections, and it's surely not in front of others. Former New York Times features columnist, author Bob Morris, author of Assisted Loving: True Tales of Double Dating With My Dad found these uninvited corrections so annoying that corrections was the subject of one of his Sunday columns. (October 21, 2007, New York Times).

Make it easy for people to save face and self-correct. "I was under the impression that it was a 2 percent increase" is better than "Where did you hear that figure? It hasn't been 4 percent in twenty years!" or "Dude, you are so off."

Let good judgement and common sense prevail, and call off the detail guards! If it doesn't really matter, let it go. I was at a holiday dinner where our gracious host was recalling the longevity of this particular historic and religious observance. A guest piped up and corrected him. I knew his historic recollection was off fifty years, but chose to say nothing. When I saw the look on my host's face after being corrected and felt the heaviness in the air, I was delighted when another guest lightened the moment by saying, "After five thousand years, it's easy to lose count!"

BUILDING A BASE FOR BUSINESS

As shocking as it may seem, people don't attend conferences, meetings, picnics or fund-raisers just so that we can promote and sell our wares to them in the face-to-face space! The tacit agreement at business functions is that it's about everyone's business—and no one signed on strictly to hear our spiel. We earn the right to our say by being part of the group dynamic and by building conversation, rapport and relationships.

If the conversation lags, we may pick it up by saying, "I joined you late, so I didn't catch your names, ranks and serial numbers. By the way, I'm Anna Karenina." It's a light, no-pressure way of asking people their names, where they work, their titles and other important information.

People often talk about the event or venue because that's common ground. The corporate golf tournament is famous for being a soft-sell venue—so much so that both men and women are learning the game. The benefits of conversation on the links are incalculable. Playing a couple of rounds with people is telltale. According to speaker and golf fanatic Mark Mayberry, "You learn a lot about people, their ethics, demeanor and attitude when you play golf."

We learn a lot from conversations when we participate and listen.

More Food for Thought

All talkers need a listener and that's a memorable contribution. We participate with our eyes, facial expressions, smiles and nods of agreement.

> This is a chance to learn something new. Interjecting "Wow!" or "Really?" is participating—as long as our enthusiasm is sincere. I often listen to "techno-nerds" discuss computers and web sites in sheer amazement, and I convey my awe at their knowledge.
>
> Just because someone else knows more than we do about a certain topic doesn't mean that we're lacking. As much as those lovable nerds know about electronic networking and motherboards, I know about personal networking and blackboards (we ex-teachers know how to chalk up a room).

An event reminder: Keep phones on vibrate, take off the Bluetooth®, take out the iPod Ear Buds, and resist checking e-mail and text messages when in a face-to-face conversation.

BEING PROVOCATIVE CAN PROVOKE

There are people who take great pride in being provocative. Several people I surveyed reported this as a technique that they've used, or had seen used, successfully. One wrote about a woman she knew who always posed questions at group functions, like, "If there were a fire, what would you save: your cat or your favorite painting?" In some groups, that may work well, but proceed with caution. People don't enjoy contrived conversational gambits, they don't like to be set up, and some topics could turn into debates.

Observing, understanding, honoring and contributing—these are the keys to good group conversational dynamics. A little charm, with a dose of chutzpah, and you, too, will shine in the face-to-face space when you're up close and personal, no matter how large the group.

ROANE'S REMINDERS

* Ninety percent or more of people in any group are nice, are raised to be polite, and have more in common than not.
* Just showing up in the face-to-face space is not enough, although it's a start.
* The person who shines in a crowd does three things:

1. Focuses on the other person(s) with whom he or she is speaking and engages each member with eye contact (up to eight seconds, after which is considered a glare)
2. Introduces others with enthusiasm and information that facilitates further conversation
3. Has three to five planned pieces of conversation

   • Prepare for each event: check your attitude, practice a seven- to nine-second self-introduction keyed to the event, and let your charm and chutzpah (courage) fly.
   • Civility and good manners are telling.
   • Leave the Bluetooth®, BlackBerry,® or iPod in your pocket.
   • Introduce yourself to those who may look familiar by saying your name and commenting that they look familiar.
   • Exercise good judgement. Observe and listen to group conversations before you contribute. Avoid derailing conversation by ill-timed funny lines.
   • Build on comments from others in the group.
   • Be inclusive. Act like the host.

Chapter Three

Don't Shy Away from This Chapter

Many people avoid face-to-face opportunities because they're part of the ninety-three percent of American adults who self-identify as shy. According to Dr. Philip Zimbardo, professor emeritus at Stanford University and one of the founders of Stanford's Shyness Clinic, while some people are situationally shy, others feel they were once shy, claim to have worked through it, and admit to the occasional relapse. Still others claim to be generally shy. And only 8 percent are phobically shy and require individual professional treatment. The strategies in this book will help push you through your social discomfort and master face-to-face situations.

A favorite television show of mine is Bravo's Inside the Actors Studio. Time and again, interviewer James Lipton reveals a trait shared by many of his guests: their admitted shyness. Yet acting classes and drama clubs gave them the opportunities and the chops for playing other characters who weren't shy. If you're shy, you're in good company with Tom Hanks, Beyoncé, Brad Pitt, Julia Roberts, Gloria Estefan, David Letterman and Albert Einstein! There are many more accomplished, smart, talented people who, like yourself, may sometimes feel shy when it comes to face-to-face interactions.

Tim Gunn, Project Runway's mentor figure and cohost of Tim Gunn's Guide to Style, revealed that he suffered from shyness and a stutter. In a Wall Street Journal feature (October 25, 2007), "Tricks of the Trade," Gunn recalled that he was "so terrified he'd brace his back against the wall [at events] in order to stand."

He got over his fear and counsels his students to "become a good actor, practice and work on overcoming shyness."

THE POINT TO REMEMBER

In every room you enter, every face-to-face situation you encounter, the majority of people feel equally uncomfortable or shy. They could be colleagues, coworkers, clients or cousins, even the CEO or you, if you're the CEO. We may think that the shy are disinterested or disengaged, snobbish, and aloof. The reality is they're just as uncomfortable as you may be.

We need to give people the benefit of the doubt. They may not be snobs; they may just be shy. We must be sure that our assessment of others as snobs isn't snobbery itself. According to the illuminating, smart and often humorous Snobbery (Houghton Mifflin Co., Boston, 2002, p. 242), by Joseph Epstein (who attended my Chicago grammar school), "The problem of snobbery in its contemporary manifestation lies not in some small number of pure snobs in the world, but in the multitudinous little snobberies that infect us all." The people who appear to be aloof just may be more uncomfortable than you are.

LET'S EMBRACE OUR INNER SHY PERSON

"We don't need less shyness in the world, we need more. Shy people are wonderful. Imagine if everyone were like Howard Stern or Madonna," said Dr. Bernardo Carducci, author of Shyness: A Bold New Approach (Psychology Today, November/December 2005, p. 30), at the American Psychological Association annual meeting. The shy among us pay attention to people; they focus on conversational partners and listen! They listen intently, focusing on the speaker, not planning their grocery list. We can see, hear and feel their attention.

While many rooms are overworked by the bon vivant, the bombastic and the braggart, the shy are none of the above. In face-to-face situations they're the people who focus on their conversation partners, listen, share ideas and offer leads. Their eyes don't dart over our shoulders and around the room to see who else is in attendance.

WHY ARE WE SHY?

A Harvard study conducted by Jerome Ragan (Psychology Today, April 2007, p. 71) indicates there is a shyness gene. However, Dr. Philip Zimbardo found, "Most people become shy as they grow up." In a 1995 article in the San Francisco Chronicle, he attributes the increase in the numbers of those who self-identify as shy to three factors:

1. Automation: we can get our money from a hole in the wall (ATM) and never see or talk to a teller.
2. Personal computers, the Internet, and home electronic entertainment: they contribute to the increase of cyber surfing, which means less social interaction.
3. Telecommuting: working at home, using the tools and toys of technology, people don't have the opportunity to chitchat at work and don't participate in the social life of their job.

In today's techie toy world, we do stay connected by e-mail, text message and tweets, which are instant messages of up to 140 characters that can be sent to friends, family or co-workers via twitter.com. Yet, according to Dr. Pelusi, "Technology often encourages us to further segregate ourselves" (Psychology Today, November/December 2007, p. 64). And that contributes to our discomfort in face-to-face social interaction.

WHAT CAN WE DO ABOUT SHYNESS?

PJ Livingston, a former client and current friend, who readily admitted that he was painfully shy as a teenager, shared, "I thought shyness was a debilitating disease because I suffered so much from it." That was a total surprise to me because PJ is outgoing, verbal, and a superb communicator. "My math teacher was the mentor who saw qualities in me I didn't know I had. Because I wanted to emulate him, he became the role model I needed."

Although PJ may have felt that his shyness was a disease, it isn't. Only 8 percent of those who are shy are considered to be socially phobic. The rest of us suffer from normal discomfort that can be remedied without medication. In Shyness: How Normal Behavior Became a Sickness, author Christopher Lane (Yale University Press, New Haven, 2007) claims that shy folks comprise "just about everyone at one time or another." In his book reviewed in the Wall Street Journal (November 3, 2007), reviewer Paul McHugh suggests a remedy for allaying the social difficulty of shy people: coaching and practice, which is what PJ began to do.

PJ studies people. He observes their carriage, demeanor and mannerisms. "I learned three big lessons from being a shy student of people:

1. Overcoming shyness is a lifetime commitment.
2. If we put people in their comfort zone, they communicate better.
3. If something doesn't work for me, I don't do it again.

I continue to study, adopt and emulate" (What Do I Say Next? Warner Books, New York, 1999, p. 451). We can do the same.

Before you leave your house or office, give yourself a positive pep talk. Review those times you've extended yourself that had good outcomes. Ninety-three percent of people are also uncomfortable and shy, so you are not alone.

THE SEVEN QUICK-STEP SHYNESS RECOVERY PROGRAM

1. Decide to recover. The ability to communicate and converse is part of business. Bosses expect it. And bosses are expected to do it.

Making the decision to overcome shyness is a good first step.

2. Observe those who are mingling mavens and ConverSENsations™. They are role models. Note what they do and say, and replicate those behaviors. As Dr. Melfi, Tony Soprano's psychiatrist, advised, "Act as if . . ." you're not shy.

3. Be approachable. Be sure your body language is open. Smile. Make eye contact. This is natural for shy people, who tend to focus on their conversation partners rather than scanning the room while engaged in conversation a meet off patting behavior, which we all must avoid.

4. Have three to five interesting news stories to discuss. While you're at it, read a newspaper, several online sites, a few books or movie reviews. Join a book club, wine club, or theater group. Do things you don't normally do so that you have something to talk about and bring to every face-to-face encounter. That's why I went rappelling once and only once baked bread. I just needed to know I could do it, and the experience gave me something to talk about.

5. Practice three to five anecdotes or stories that happened to you or others. It might be something funny, provocative or ear-catching. Feel free to borrow from other people's lives—and remember to save the punch line for last. Make sure the punch line is never at the expense of someone else so that it sounds like a put-down.

6. Take an acting, improvisation, or conversation class. You'll meet other people who may be shy and you'll learn to take risks in safe settings.

7. Practice. Smile. Say hello and talk to people along all paths of life: the bridle path, the bike path, the track, the grocery line, and in the elevator. Bite the bullet, take the risk, and say something. You'll be pleasantly surprised. People respond in kind 90 percent of the time.

SO YOU THINK YOU CAN DANCE AWAY SHYNESS?

The answer is yes. After speaking to a group of information technology professionals, computer geeks and security people, a young techie told me his secret: "I'm one of those shy people you talked about and a former hacker. To help me overcome my shyness, I'm taking ballroom dance lessons." Mastering moves on the dance floor is building his confidence. He's in a group situation with other adults who share the same interest, so they have a common bond and launching pad for partnered and group conversations.

According to a study at the University of London, patients with anxiety disorders who attended a modern dance class were the only group that reduced their anxiety. An exercise, music or math class didn't have the same effect, according to Elizabeth Svoboda in an article in Psychology Today (April 2007, p. 62). An Italian study for cardiac rehab showed the same results for a waltzing class. According to the Dance Therapy Association, dancing bonds people who like to move to music.

I take Latin aerobics dance classes three times a week, an African tribal dance class, and an occasional hip-hop class. It's challenging, as we have to remember choreography while we raise our heart rates, whether we're moving to Marc Anthony, Chris Brown or Rihanna. It's so much fun that our dance class community has bonded. We've become a really social network of people who see each other outside the health club. After reading research on the brain benefits of dance class, I clipped the article and gave it to my instructor. Yes, we're dancing away dementia, pounds and shyness!

Taking steps, dance or otherwise, to join a group of people with common interests is a good move. Whether it's rock climbing, book reading, cooking, kayaking, running, wine tasting, or any club of your choosing, you'll already have interests in common that are subjects for conversation.

What's important to remember is that 93 percent of us identify as shy in certain situations. If you're part of this group, you have a lot of good company! And that can lead to good connected face-to-face (F2F) conversations. If it's uncomfortable approaching a group already in conversation, focus on meeting the people who are standing alone. They would welcome your hello. It would be very kind and gracious to notice the person who is alone and extend yourself to him or her.

Hot Tip

Worth repeating. Focus on making other people comfortable with you. No one knows better than a shy person how daunting face-to-face interaction can be. Having a goal to make others comfortable allows you to be the host and takes the spotlight and pressure off you.

ROANE'S REMINDERS

* Ninety-three percent of American adults self-identify as shy.
* Shy people are generally good listeners who pay attention to their conversation partners.
* Observe people who are at ease in face-to-face situations. Try to imitate some of their behaviors.
* Be approachable. Make eye contact and smile.
* Read newspapers and have three to five interesting stories to share.
* Take an acting, improvisation or dance class.
* Say yes to social opportunities and business events.
* Practice, practice, practice—even if you don't intend to get to Carnegie Hall.

Chapter Four

Talk Targets: Becoming a Magnet

Talk Targets are people with whom it's easy to make conversation, whether it's on the phone or in person. Not only are they comfortable, skilled, and adept at small talk, they effortlessly segue to big talk and back again to small talk. They are inclusive, engaging, interesting and interested, and they make us feel at ease as they open us up without being invasive. If you've ever complimented someone on her conversational prowess and she looked at you and said, "But I only talk easily and say clever things around you!"—you're the Talk Target.

Being a Talk Target who turns other people into good conversationalists is a gift that we can all learn. Talk Targets bring their personal touch to our space as they share, motivate, and encourage communication that builds relationships and business. We find them at work, at home, on sports fields, in meetings or classrooms, in lines at the company cafeteria or local supermarkets, everywhere we encounter people. Talk Targets are aware that people have feelings and respond to words, so they choose them wisely.

This chapter is about the secrets of Talk Targets, how they put their gift to work, and what we can learn from them to improve our interpersonal communication in any room. Talk Targets are not self-absorbed. They think about other people's comfort, issues and feelings. They're not people who we would characterize as entitled, a pejorative term that describes people who think the world revolves around them. We all know people like that, and that's something I never want said about me.

> **Hot Tip**
>
> Talk Targets know it's not what you say, but how you make people feel when you say it.

TALK TARGETS "SALE" ALONG

It's easy to buy from and do business with Talk Targets. They make in-person sales calls that get results. Sales organizations and companies have been built on the success of the face-to-face house call from door-to-door salespeople. The Fuller Brush Company and Avon were built on the personal touch. In a Wall Street Journal interview (October 15, 2007, p. B1), Andrea Jung, CEO of Avon, said that door-to-door sales still works. "Things have changed in many ways but one thing hasn't—the need for personalized service." The entire direct sales industry is based on face-to-face interaction with Talk Targets who know their products and services and provide first-line customer service.

Michael Hirsch, vice president of Chia, occasionally spends a week in New York calling on his clients. "So much more happens when we're having an in-person conversation, whether it's at their office or at a restaurant. Some of my contacts at client firms have either moved on or retired. Doing my sales calls gives me an opportunity to meet and connect with the new person." Hirsch is a ConverSensation™ who is a true Talk Target. Known as Mr. Chia Pet, the name of his well-known product, Michael travels the world to bring his person and personal touch to every client.

Lee, a senior consultant with a major consulting firm that serves Fortune 100 companies, finally landed an appointment with the chief financial officer of a big firm. "I had been warned that this guy was a tough hombre, a man of few words who liked to get right to the point. That made me a bit uncomfortable, but I saw a photo of a beautiful boat on his desk, so I asked if he sailed. He said yes, and he asked if I did. 'I wish I did,' I said. 'But I parasail and am sporting a bruise from my last outing.' He asked how it happened, so I told him and said, 'Let me show you.'" The tough hombre relaxed, chatted easily about sailing, and ultimately gave Lee his business. Lee had hit upon a topic of importance to his client and was willing to risk sharing and showing bruises.

Lee is a Talk Target who used the OAR™ approach to maneuver what could have been rough waters. He:

- Observed the photo
- Asked about it with interest
- Revealed his own sport and the bruises he sported.

Lee also gave his potential client some information to which the man could respond. That built the conversation that gave Lee the business. What if Lee had followed some of the mirroring advice and changed his style of conversation to adapt to the tough hombre of few words? He may or may not have landed the client, but he wouldn't have established the rapport that has made their business arrangement a pleasant relationship.

Talk Targets give people information on which to hang their conversation. Dawne Bernhardt, speech coach, says, "I don't wait. When I say my name, I add something the other person can hook into in order to build a conversation." He takes the bait and the conversation begins. Because Dawne travels a lot, she may mention that she just returned from a trip to Vietnam, Vienna, or Vermont. That gives other people enough information to make a comment or ask a question, and the exchange begins. One of her friends said that Dawne could strike up a conversation with a tombstone! But she prefers not to.

TALK TARGETS LISTEN

Terry Norton, another Talk Target and co-owner of an upscale frame shop, finds that face-to-face in-depth conversation with customers is critical to success. "That's how we learn about our customers so we can meet their needs. By the time I've designed the framing for their family portrait, I can recite their favorite family legends and name both sets of grandparents. My clients, because they've been treated well and listened to, walk out of my gallery as my least expensive marketing tool—an enthusiastic referral. You can project any image you choose in a business conversation, but if you're insincere, you risk being perceived as a phony."

The importance of focused listening cannot be overemphasized.

AND THEY REFER

Talk Targets listen to colleagues, coworkers, employees, clients, and friends. Like Joanne Black, author of No More Cold Calling™ (Warner Business Books, New York, 2006), they will not only effortlessly recommend but follow up to be sure you have the information you need, as she recently did for me. She embodies the spirit and message of referrals so that we don't have to make cold calls. Joanne suggests to her audiences and readers that they attend one networking event a week in order to meet new people, increase their referral base, and develop business relationships.

> ### Hot Tip
> Talk Targets are sincere, never disingenuous. You'll never hear them say, "How can I help you?" as a setup for requesting your business, support or referrals. They offer ideas, information and suggestions without an ounce of strategic thinking or self-interest.

Talk Targets observe people and assess situations to see what will make for the most enjoyable and productive conversations. If those Talk Targets happen to be in sales, they're bound to succeed.

FIT TO BE TIED

Talk Targets go out of their way to make people feel comfortable. My brother Michael was the head attorney for a Chicago city department and served on the school board of his community. He often wears Save Our Children™ ties that are designed by kids. They are distinctive, eye-catching and fun, plus a portion of the profits go to the organization. "Wearing a tie with big yellow school buses or children on the school yard lets people know that it's okay to approach me when I conduct an open community meeting. It gives them something to talk about and also gives them a chance to feel good about initiating the conversation." Michael is a lifelong Three Stooges fan. So I bought him a tie with Moe, Curly and Larry that says, "Dewey, Cheatem and Howe, Attorneys at Law." That definitely makes him approachable and soitainly gives people something to start the conversation. I'll have to check to see if his answers are concluded with, "Nyuk, Nyuk."

More and more men are wearing Disney, Looney Tunes, South Park, Jerry Garcia Collection, and other fun ties. They're conversation openers and one of the few fashion options for men in the corporate world. When we see someone with an unusual or fun tie, he's inviting conversation. Take him up on the invitation.

We can invite conversation with anything that's fun, bright, or unusual—a brooch, a lapel pin, earrings, or a brightly colored scarf. The inherent message we're giving is, "I'm approachable." Patricia Fripp professional speaker and speech coach, often wears stunning, dramatic hats that invite comment. When asked why she wears hats, her answer is always, "So I can meet interesting people like you," and she does.

GET THE MESSAGE

The skill of hearing what is being said—and not said—requires an uncanny ability to comprehend. Because we have different language patterns and customs across the country, as well as glob-ally, that can be difficult. Dr. Deborah Tannen first highlighted her findings on geographic communication patterns in That's Not What I Meant (Ballantine Books, New York, 1987).

In an episode of FX's The Shield, the female district attorney shows up at the precinct asking for a specific file. "May I please have the file?" The detective replies, "Sure," and continues to stay seated. The district attorney walks over to the detective's desk, changes her tone, and says, "I'm from the South and I was raised to be polite. Don't misconstrue it. That wasn't a question. If you don't get me that file now, I will have this precinct closed in twenty-four hours." The detective gets up, goes to the file cabinet, finds the file, and hands it to the DA. She turns to him and returns to the same polite tone as she says, "Thank you very much."

"Thank you very much" is the signature phrase for Emmy Award–winning Kyra Sedgewick's character, Brenda Johnson, in The Closer. In an episode, her boss turns to Brenda and asks, "May I see you in my office?" "Right now I have to . . ." she re-sponds. The Chief cuts her off and says, "Let me rephrase that rhetorical question." He changes his tone and turns the question into an imperative sentence: "I want to speak with you . . . now."

Paying attention to people's communication styles pays off.

AVOID BLUNT TRAUMA

Talk Targets and good communicators have well-developed filter-ing systems. Much like the ones we install to purify our water, these also keep out the gunk. Talk Targets don't offer unsolicited opinions about things you never asked them to assess. You'll never hear them say, "I'm Frank," unless that's their first name.

A friend decided to tell me just what she thought of a com-munication I had had with my medical provider. When I said she was the only one who assessed it as such, her slightly indignant response was, "I'm entitled to my opinion." The first amendment guarantees the right to free speech. But I didn't ask for her opinion. Just because we think something, doesn't mean it has to come out of our mouth. It was negative gunk. We need to prevent blunt trauma by filtering our thoughts before they come out of our mouth.

Talk Targets self-assess and self-censure. To paraphrase author Elmore Leonard, "I don't write what people won't read." The Talk Target doesn't say what people don't need to hear.

To communicate well in person or on the phone is a skill, even a gift. And it's a gift we can give ourselves by adding a rhetorical question to our self-talk. Before we say (or do) something, we should ask ourselves, "What would be the point?" That question is one that my best friend, Lana Teplick, has asked me when I've run many situations by her. If the point is good, I proceed. If I can't articulate a good point, I drop it. Corollaries to her question were provided by Sherwood Cummins personal trainer and owner of recreate, "What do you expect or want? Is what you're going to say or do going to get you there?" Keeping this trio of questions in mind will contribute to effective communication in all face-to-face situations.

UNDIVIDED ATTENTION

What could be more flattering than the person who gives his or her undivided attention? Whether it's a friend, a coworker, a colleague or a parent, spouse, son, or sister, listening to someone without distraction sends a message. In a televised service, Pastor Joel Osteen, author of Your Best Life Now (FaithWords, Nashville, 2004) and Become a Better You (Simon & Schuster, New York, 2007), said that the message we send when we focus on others is, "You're important to me."

When we're with people and we allow ourselves to be distracted, we send the opposite message: "You aren't that important." Talk Targets don't do that.

TELEPHONE TALK TARGETS

Over the phone, our voice has to do double duty, communicating facial expression and body language, as well as tone. The best telephone Talk Targets are easy, confident conversationalists who never come off as scripted, even if they're making a sales call and have notes in front of them. They're experts at turning as a cold call—calling someone they don't know in order to make a connection or sale—into a warm call. But their secrets for connection and success apply to all calls, both business and personal.

To engage people on the phone, we have to treat them as if we already know them, and then we can appropriately share a bit of ourselves to give them information on which to build. The catch is that we can't be presumptuous, and we must be respectful.

The Enormous Benefits of Being a Telephone Talk Target

- Getting and giving information
- Connecting with a contact
- Developing rapport
- Building business
- Learning something
- Solving problems
- Making a friend

I was fortunate to give a program on How to Work a Room® for the University of Hawaii at Manoa. Because he thought the program would be beneficial to his colleagues, a local insurance salesperson suggested that I call Marcie Bannon, then a program director for the National Association of Professional Insurance Agents. I did, and over two to three years we developed a telephone friendship. She didn't hire me to speak for her convention that year, or for the next two, but we stayed in touch because we liked talking to each other. Eventually, Marcie did hire me to speak for PIA, where we met for the first time. Our phone conversations had laid the groundwork. What began as a short phone chat has grown into a two-decade-long friendship.

If I hadn't followed up on the suggestion to call Marcie, I not only wouldn't have had the chance to speak to her association and to be the recipient of her support and her industry advice over the years, I would have missed out on a special friendship. Would this all have happened with a virtual introduction and conversations conducted on the keyboard? Possibly, but not likely.

TALK TARGETS KNOW WHEN TO FOLD 'EM

Talk Targets hear, observe and intuit on the phone and in person other people's exit cues, whether it's a lull in the conversation, eyes roaming the room, body language that shows impatience, papers being shuffled, the keyboard being used in the background or a shifting or drifting voice. On the phone, Talk Targets respond to the cue with phrases like, "Thanks for your time. I know you're busy. I should let you go. Take care. Good-bye." In face-to-face situations, they exit gracefully by extending their hand for the good-bye handshake and saying, "It's been so good (fun, interesting) to talk to you about Wimbledon and who will win this year." Then they walk about a quarter of the room away to someone else, join an in-progress group or go noshing at the buffet table.

TALKING WITH OUR FACES

The expressionless face is as uninspiring as a monotone delivery. The most compelling conversational partner I've ever encountered listened with his face. He wasn't afraid to make faces. I could see the surprise, the empathy, the awe, the "oh, wow!" When he spoke, his face matched his words. While it was seductive to talk to such an animated person, it was also educational.

He inspired me to allow myself to talk with my face. And its a point I share with my audiences: when our facial expressions match our words, we're more interesting.

SENTENCE SENSE

Whether it's face to face or in cyberspace, the types of sentences we use in e-mails, letters, or conversations make an impression. To be sure it's a good one, let's go back to basics for a moment. There are four types of sentences:

1. Declarative sentences make a statement. For example, "The mail rebates are more trouble than they're worth."
2. Interrogative sentences ask a question. For example, "Have you had problems receiving your rebates?"
3. Imperative sentences issue a command (you is the understood subject). For example, "Fill in the rebate form."
4. Exclamatory sentences express surprise. For example, "I can't believe my rebate came in less than two weeks!"

Clear, brief and to the point, imperative sentences generally come across as commands or fit the category of barked orders. Talk Targets don't do this. Consider using imperative sentences sparingly in print, whether in a letter, an e-mail or text message, as well as in face-to-face personal interactions.

THE MAGIC WORDS

If we attended kindergarten, we've heard the phrase "the magic words." Our parents, teachers and coaches reminded us when and how to use them. And we pass on the lesson as we teach them to the next generation. Talk Targets use certain magic words again and again, each time with sincerity, interest and genuine connection. We can emulate them to increase our interpersonal prowess. Every year, new magic words and expressions are added to our lexicon, and some may sail off into the sunset. Some of the magic arrows in the Talk Target's conversational quivers are:

- "Please."
- "What a great tie!"
- "Hello" or "Hi" or "Hey!"
- "Oops! I forgot."
- "You played a great game (round, match, set)."
- "What can I do for you?"
- "I'm proud of you."
- "Excuse me."
- "How may I help?"
- "Congratulations!"
- "So sorry," or, "I do apologize." ("My bad" is cute, but not an appropriate apology.)
- "What's going on?"
- "Have a good weekend."
- "How was the golf tournament (or bowling tournament or cure-a-thon)?"
- "No, thank you."
- "How are you?" (And they listen to the answer.)
- "Good morning."
- "Good idea!"
- "Cool."
- "May I?"
- "Sweet."
- "Would it work for you?"
- "I'd appreciate a call back," or "It'd be great to hear from you," or "Give me a call."
- "Wow! That's fantastic."
- "Pardon me for interrupting . . ."
- "You're welcome."
- "No problem." (This is not a substitute for "You're welcome," but may work in combination with it.)
- "I could use your help."

- "Happy to help."
- "Good presentation."
- "Great job."
- "I'd be happy to." (You could add, "It's my pleasure.")
- "How did it go?"
- "You can do this."
- "Kind of you to offer."
- "You must be pleased, (proud, happy)."
- "Thank you."

Recognize them? They're all words that show courtesy, respect and consideration for others, and they are the core of polite, interested, supportive communication. Some also show praise and others encouragement. Some of the phrases sound formal, but there's no underestimating the effect of these magic words. There are other similar expressions that you can add to the list. Though we learned these expressions early in life, they're even more important now. How we say them is equally important. Demetrius Greer is a client and firmwide director of attorney recruiting at Paul, Hastings Janofsky and Walker, LLP. He attends many social and community events and finds that "being polite is imperative." He doesn't just recommend it for others; he lives his message, which I experienced firsthand.

In an interview, Matt Damon, an actor known for being nice even to the paparazzi (Parade Magazine, September 2, 2007), mentioned revering Mickey Rourke, who gave him very sage advice. "Don't do what I did. Show up on time and be polite to everyone." Matt Damon took Mickey Rourke's advice to heart. So can we.

With so many newspaper and magazine articles in the last few years addressing civility, or the lack of it, being considered polite and civil are good things. We spend millions of dollars a year on training and retraining, as well as for seminars on managing and motivating, so that people can work harder, better, and smarter. Yet research has shown that what people really want is to be acknowledged and feel appreciated. We could save a lot of money just by making the magic words please and thank you part of our conversation cachet, whether we say them, type them, or text them. While some may say this use—or lack of use—of these phrases, civility and manners is generational, that isn't true. The good news is that we all can emulate Talk Targets regardless of our generational designation. Try the phrases. The responses may surprise and please you. According to Psychology Today (March/April 2006), feeling thankful and expressing that thanks makes us feel happier and healthier. And it does wonders for the people being thanked.

Being polite, respectful and appreciative is never a waste of time; it's an investment. I've never heard anyone say, "My boss is such a jerk; she complimented me on my project design." It may sound simplistic, but it's the little things in life that count and contribute to the conversations of life.

THE THANKLESS JOB

Not consistently using the magic words can cost more than we might know. "Dr. Kaye" was an assistant school superintendent of personnel in a local school district. Six months after he re-placed a well-liked administrator, one of his secretarial staff told me, "Dr. Kaye never thanks anyone for anything. Whatever we do goes unnoticed."

A mutual associate wanted the new assistant superintendent to succeed and not to be sabotaged by his staff, so she shared the comment. Dr. Kaye's response was, "Why should I thank them for doing what's in their job descriptions?" No wonder his em-ployees all thought they had "thankless jobs"!

Dr. Kaye wasn't shy; he had plenty to say to his peers and to the people whose votes he needed for projects, for funding, and for his contract. But his local school district stay was short-lived. No surprise there. An educator with a Ph.D. in human resources should've known better how to value, communicate and motivate his own office staff.

TALK TARGETS MAKE IT SAFE

We can only build in-depth connections when people trust us. They must feel safe in order to share deeper, more important, and more intimate thoughts, ideas, goals, and plans, whether the conversation is personal or professional. They need to know that their confidence won't be betrayed or misused. That kind of trust builds over the course of time as does the relationship.

If we're the ones sharing confidences, we should be careful about the "I'm truthful, I tell all, I let it all hang out" school of sharing. When we're "in our truth," we may be taking care of ourselves at the expense of others—using them as dump sites or unpaid therapists. Talk Targets don't do that. As I read a Men's Health article (June 16, 2006) on "old-school rules," I could just see my father as the man they extolled. "Old school values privacy as a priority. Old school is not big on sharing." Verbal dumping can be just as off-putting as people who share little about themselves. We need to take our cues from others, honor their boundaries, and not spill our guts if it isn't appropriate.

OBSERVING IRONY

Observing the irony in situations lends itself to good humor as well as to a good story. When Bonnie Edwards suggested we try a new local restaurant, I agreed. I later learned it was a vegan raw-food restaurant, which was fine. When we arrived, I looked over the menu and my eyes must have turned to saucers. There was nothing I found appealing, so I settled on a salad. Fortunately, I wasn't too hungry, or so I thought. When I asked for butter to go with the ersatz cracker (yes, I prefer real unsalted butter to slather on my food), my friend reminded me it was a vegan restaurant. Okay, when in Rome . . .

I admit I don't have a poker face, which is why I'm not a card player. Sadly, my lack of poker face sometimes plays out at the food table. When I am thrilled, it's visible. When I'm not, I try to control my expression. Bonnie had raved about the delicious coffee, so I couldn't wait to have a cup. When I ordered their delicious coffee, decaffeinated, the waitress looked at me and said, "We don't serve decaf." The irony didn't escape me. I laughed out loud, thinking, "You mean that a vegan raw-food health-food restaurant only serves coffee with caffeine?" Irony is everywhere.

Although I thought I wasn't hungry, Bonnie did mention that when we were at the show, I ate all the popcorn! I've shared this story in a number of conversations that have to do with restaurants and food in general. When I tell this story, my tone, inflection and timing match the content. By the way, while writing this chapter, I did a perception check with Bonnie about my expressions during dinner. She assured me that my efforts at maintaining a poker face worked, although I can't imagine how.

EXPRESSIONS OF GRIEF

Talk Targets know what to say in difficult situations. While it's sometimes uncomfortable to have a conversation with a person in crisis or mourning and we may not know what to say, it's important to express support, sympathy and concern, and perhaps to give a gentle sympathetic touch. Not to do so speaks volumes about a person—and it's not positive.

I recently bumped into a woman who I've known for years from aerobics classes. When I saw her face, I could tell something was awry, so I asked what was going on. Sharon explained that one of her best friends had just died of cancer. "I feel like I lost a part of me. It hurts; I'm so sad. Our families were so close."

It wasn't easy to respond with what felt like the right words. I touched her outer upper arm and said, "You've suffered a great loss, a best friend. I am so sorry to hear of her death. This must be so heartbreaking for you." Her grief was available, visible and palpable. We give our sympathies and condolences to family members of those who have passed away, yet we often forget those who are the "family of friends" who can experience grief as well.

"I didn't say anything because I didn't know what to say" is, at best, a flimsy excuse. People have told me that they've felt ignored or abandoned by friends and colleagues who "didn't know what to say," so they said and did nothing. Talk Targets know that we have to take the focus off ourselves and place it on the person who is in pain. This requires empathy and sympathy, even if we can only say, "I just don't know what to say, but my thoughts are with you." Bosses, clients, coworkers and friends lose spouses, siblings, offspring, parents and friends. There is much to be learned from "old-school" people. They go to funerals, pay their respects, and even say a few words (Men's Health, September 2006).

Even when we honestly feel too overwhelmed to respond to people who have experienced an accident, illness, operation, or death, there are online and in-print greeting cards for every occasion. We can at least, let people know we're thinking of them, and we may get an idea of what to say from perusing the cards.

Hot Tip
While we can send an online sympathy card, the one that you mail can be reread, saved and displayed as we do with holiday cards. Their visibility can offer ongoing condolences and comfort.

Caution: Saying, "I know how you feel," is a slippery slope, unless you have endured similar circumstances. A thirty-five-year-old widow told me how upsetting it was to be told that by someone whose ninety-one-year-old grandmother had died. "We had just buried my forty-year-old husband who left two young sons. Nothing could be more different." I learned from her to say, "I can't imagine how you must feel," or " . . . how difficult this must be."

Expressions of Grief

- "I'm so sorry to hear of your loss."
- "It's so difficult to lose a good friend (parent, spouse, child)."
- "I don't know what to say."
- "I can't imagine it."
- "Please accept my sympathies."
- "How may I help?"

During my presentation for a Coca-Cola leadership conference, one of the attendees mentioned that just asking or offering help in times of illness or loss is not enough. "Most people won't call and tell you what they need. So I decided to do something and not wait to be asked when my good friend was undergoing chemotherapy. I organized all of our friends to provide meals for the family, so it was one thing they didn't have to be concerned with. And for the two years that she lived, we alternated preparing and delivering the dinners to the family." After she sat down, the entire audience applauded her and more than a few wiped away tears.

Being a Talk Target requires emotional intelligence, especially in difficult times. We don't have to say much, but we do have to be sincere. People appreciate our sympathy and empathy, and they know when it's real.

Hot Tip

When attending a memorial, a funeral, a wake, or making a condolence call, leave your Bluetooth™ in your pocket. Wearing it negates the purpose of paying respects. And don't check your BlackBerry or Treo during the service.

You may wonder why I included this hot tip, as it seems to be obvious. I've done so because each of those misbehaviors has come to my attention as they have occurred. I wish I could say I made them up, but that's not so.

THE MANTRA OF MODERATION

At the heart of Talk Targets' success is their ability to maintain balance. Anything can be a problem when taken to the extreme. The ability to balance and moderate our conversations shows up in many ways. These are some of the paradoxes that Talk Targets have mastered:

- Being open, but not too open
- Being silent to listen, but not too silent
- Being sympathetic, but not cloying
- Being of good energy without overwhelming people
- Being a talker and teller of stories without monopolizing the conversation

Knowing what to say, and when and how to say it, is crucial. We can develop these skills by taking the time to be attuned to others. That's the secret of Talk Targets' success.

Don't Do As Talk Targets Don't Do

While there is much we can learn to do from Talk Targets of all ages, we can also learn what they don't do or say when face to face. Talk Targets do not:

- Speak to compete
- Interrupt and change the focus of the conversation to themselves
- Correct other people's grammar
- Use put-down humor
- "One up" people
- Tell insensitive, off-color jokes

> - Hog the floor
> - Contradict people during a group conversation
> - Look over our shoulders to scan the scene while speaking to us

INCONTROVERTIBLE TALK TIPS

What Talk Targets do to make others feel comfortable and encourage conversation in the face-to-face space are things we can all do and say. Here's a partial list developed from the questionnaire I designed for the one hundred ConverSensations™ I interviewed.

- Take the first step and initiate. Say hello.
- Listen to introductions. Good listening requires practice and silence.
- Make introductions that share enough information about each person so that people want to talk to each other.
- Include others with eye contact, being sure to smile.
- Use humor appropriately to lighten conversation.
- Consider what's said and address it. Let the situation set the agenda.
- Be well read and familiar with current events.
- Have a broad range of topics of interest to discuss.
- Encourage others to contribute.
- Volley the conversation by answering questions with a comment and a return question.
- Learn about the perspectives, background, and regional conversation patterns of others.
- Shake hands web to web (no limp jellyfish or hamburger-mashing handshakes).
- Converse with an aura of authority and expertise.
- Ask opinions of others.
- Tell interesting stories.
- Be open to change and exchange.

- Be enthusiastic.
- Use others' names in conversation (but don't overuse them).
- Refrain from monopolizing conversation.
- Use varied tones, inflections, and pacing.
- Pay attention to what's been said and respond accordingly.
- Put people at ease with friendliness.
- Open up the circle of conversation by physically stepping back and allowing people to join.
- Use animated facial expressions that match your words. ("I'm so happy for you" should look and sound as if you are.)

We all do these things, and we can consciously do more of them to create and bring our personal touch to the face-to-face space.

ROANE'S REMINDERS

* Talk Targets build rapport and interpersonal communication in face-to-face situations.
* Talk Targets have unfailing good manners and make liberal use of magic words like "Please," "Thank you," "You're welcome," "Excuse me," and "Congratulations!"
* They use ice melters to spark conversation (fun ties, T-shirts, earrings, etc.) and respond when others do the same.
* They talk to those in grief and express sympathy.
* They treat the telephone as a friend that links them to others.
* They use the phone as a follow-up to online connecting.
* Talk Targets are always conscious of making it easy and comfortable for others.

Chapter Five

The Meal Deal

There will always be the business meal, whether it's breakfast, lunch or dinner. It's an opportunity to meet a potential client, colleague or coworker "off-campus" face to face. We get to break bread, share information, and have conversations that don't revolve around or take place in the office. And, hopefully, we're relaxed and uninterrupted, except by the server. It's an opportunity for people to see our body language, hear our tone and read our facial expressions.

The beauty of inviting or being invited by a peer, client or coworker to meet for any meal is that you have a chance to converse on neutral territory to get to know people and connect on a deeper level. Because people are too busy to have the three-hour lunch, with or without the celebrated martinis of yesteryear, the meal that is increasing in popularity is the business breakfast. It precedes the day, doesn't necessitate a break in work flow and has a time framework. Knowing how to make the most of your limited time in a casual atmosphere is key.

PDAS—PUBLIC DISPLAYS OF AFFECTATION

With today's technology and ETSI (Escalating Toys of Self-Importance), having an uninterrupted meal is often not the case. I wrote about ETSI a decade and a half ago when cell phones were in their infancy. Now ETSI usage, or misusage, is so prevalent that our bad gadget behavior is the norm, and it still backfires.

We now dine at restaurants where cell phones ring, and people talk to others at their table and to the caller. One morning I was having a business breakfast interview with a local newspaper reporter when we heard another patron speaking very loudly. He had a bad connection on his cell phone and regressed to long-distance phone techniques used by my grandfather—shouting to enhance the connection! Of course, this man's business was very important . . . to him! But these PDAs (public displays of affectation) are, at best, questionable, and the word rude comes to mind. Some restaurants forbid the use of cell phones in the dining area as do many private clubs—and for good reason. People don't want their meals to be disturbed by ringers, music, or shouting of conversations into a cell phone.

Phone conversations during a meal are power plays that make an impression—but not necessarily a good one. They're an excellent method for treating your host, guest, or companions as second best. It is a compliment when someone turns off his or her cell phone to focus on us. That makes for a positive personal touch in this digital world.

However, there are exceptions: the heart surgeon who learns that a donor heart is now available for a transplant . . . or the person receiving the transplant.

A Change of Heart

I never imagined I would think this, much less include it in a book, but sometimes the use of cell phones in a restaurant is not intrusive. Before a speaking engagement in Washington, D.C., I had breakfast at Kramer Books' Afterwords Café, one of my capitol rituals. It wasn't crowded, and dining al fresco was perfect. There was a table of three who were having an animated, fun and sometimes loud conversation. When they left, it was considerably quieter. Enter Jacqueline Baly Chaumette of Houston. She sat at a nearby table making business phone calls. I watched her as she spoke with varying expressions, but her voice never carried. I couldn't eavesdrop!

I would suggest that if a person is dining alone, as many

businesspeople do, it's okay to have a quiet cell phone conversation (emphasis on quiet). Is that really worse than the loud group? I think not. I've been the lone diner on the road who finds a cell phone call to a friend, client, or relative to be a great meal companion before the food arrives or later with a cup of coffee. Just be sure to have your cell phone on vibrate rather than the intrusive ring tone.

THE MEAL MEETING

When we agree to a meeting that happens over a meal, we give our tacit approval to social conversation prior to the "meat of the matter"; otherwise, we would schedule the meeting in an office, over the phone or we would e-mail. Remember, there's always time to converse, build rapport, and develop your relationship with the other person. Increasingly, this is the stuff of which business is made.

As always, preparation and planning are key. Use this six-point plan to manage the meal deal:

RoAne's Six-Point Plan for the Face-to-Face Meal Deal

1. Be prepared.
2. Know the company. Read its corporate literature, visit its Web site, and read its financial reports or Google the company.
3. Prepare conversation: a mixture of observations, questions, revelations, and vignettes from the newspaper and industry chatter.
4. Listen, listen, listen (sit on your hands if you have to!).
5. Respond accordingly.
6. Remember etiquette and the manners of doing business and meals.

You may wonder what sitting on your hands has to do with listening. A mentor advised Kayla Cohen and several colleagues to do just that. If we talk with our hands, sitting on them keeps us from interrupting, ergo, we listen better. It works.

Who Is Host?

The person who extends the invitation is the host, unless it's clear that the meal is Dutch treat, which is often the case among coworkers or colleagues. The host is the person who made the date and, therefore, picks up the tab, especially if he or she will be picking the brain of the guests, thanking them for business or hoping to connect for future business. If you use lunch as an opportunity for obtaining consultation, brainstorming or advice, you pay. It doesn't matter who earns more; what counts is that the person who shares his or her time and information is the guest.

RoAne's Rule: He or she who picks brain, picks up check.

Megameals and Deals

The host is in control of the location, agenda and conversation. If you extend the invitation, you make the plans. Of course, you check with your guest about food preferences/allergies. In the business world, picking up the tab is the power position. Some people exercise this right with such great warmth, charm and pa-nache that the guest is made to feel comfortable. With others, the power plays exceed the panache.

Some hosts control the conversation by asking questions so that the guest does all the talking/revealing, and the host contributes little to the communication. This practice may come from an old warning: "Don't talk about yourself." An attendee at one of my book events told me that he asks a lot of questions because he's afraid he'll talk too much. But then he, not the chef, becomes the griller.

The best business/social conversationalist uses the OAR method mentioned in Chapter Two:

Observe:
- "The decor is tasteful."
- "The view of the bay is magnificent!" (I live in San Francisco.)

- "There seems to be ample street parking." (This statement is purely wishful thinking in San Francisco and other metropolitan areas!)
- "The food is delicious—such unique combinations . . . mussels and kumquats."

Ask:

- "Have you been here before?"
- "How is the food?"
- "What would you recommend?"

Reveal:

- "I always like to try new restaurants where the food is ample."
- "I prefer to stay with trusted, reliable restaurants I know."
- "It took me thirty minutes to get a cab in this rain!"

Since the beginning of time, food has been more talked about than eaten. Remember the first bite of the apple? Now we discuss cholesterol, calories, grams, presentation, flavor, and so on—all food for thought and conversation.

Small talk is a good start (the restaurant, food, traffic, parking, sports teams, movies, latest gadgets). Sometimes the newest techie toy is a terrific conversation starter. At a lunch in New York in July 2007, my editor and Zach Schisgal, and I were seated in close proximity to another table. About two minutes after the other diners were seated, one of them pulled out his latest acquisition— the new I-phone—and the show-and-tell began. It led to other subjects and the conversation was on.

Keeping Tabs

Sherris Goodwin, is currently manager of resources and training for the Children's Council of San Francisco. She remembers the period of her life when she owned the Fay Mansion Inn, a popular bed-and-breakfast in San Francisco, and many other properties. "That was a time when picking up a $2,000 tab for dinner and drinks was routine. My then associates and friends expected I'd always pay, and frankly, so did I!

"I'll never forget the morning I was having breakfast with a new business associate and friend who, though struggling in her new business, picked up the tab. I was so surprised. Nobody had done that in years. It was a generous, thoughtful gesture which made me realize that, while to the other friends I was a meal ticket, to her I was a person. And we are now the best of friends."

Hot Tip

The person of means needn't always pick up the tab.

An Ounce of Prevention

In the Wall Street Journal (June 8, 2007), Jeffrey Zaslow addressed the issue of the "we want free advice crowd," because it's a growing issue among professionals. Some people will even say, "I'd like to get together to pick your brain." The picture that comes to mind is still disconcerting . . . they're going to pick out the good gray matter, and I'll be left without.

When I was asked to be the luncheon speaker for a symposium on plastic surgery, I learned of a major issue the doctors face (not the cost of malpractice insurance). They were often asked for free advice in social settings, and they wanted to have a response that was clear but not contentious. I suggested that they look at the person and say, "This light doesn't do you justice. Here's my card. Why don't you make an appointment to come to my office?" If people solicit free advice, consider having a planned response to these requests that works for you.

A Nicer Touch

I am open to spending ten to fifteen minutes on the phone with a prospective speaker, career changer, or author who has been given my name by someone in my network. Listening and sharing is important, as well as giving back. A clever, charitable alternative to being paid was shared by a local stockbroker. He will ask,

"Have my leads and ideas been helpful?" (The answer is yes.) "Is it worth a lunch?" "Sure, I'll take you to lunch." "Thanks. I don't need the calories, but here's an alternative. Send me a check made out to St. Anthony's Dining Room (or charity of choice) for what the lunch would have cost. Let's take the ideas I shared and feed some hungry people." "That's a great idea!" is always the response.

It is a win-win. You give ten to fifteen minutes of support, ideas and leads; the caller benefits; you both help feed the hungry; and, that feels really good!

Lunch 2.0

A new meal mode has come to town that combines business, social networking, and face-to-face interaction. It's been dubbed a "meal mooch," which allows people to meet, share ideas and food, and converse. Lunch 2.0 was started by accident in a Silicon Valley company cafeteria and is spreading to other cities and countries. It draws IT people, engineers, and some venture capitalists and "talent scouts." The host company provides the sustenance (often pizza) and the Lunch 2.0 crowd provides the substance. Conversations are the special meal on the menu. The global spread of this Silicon Valley phenom demonstrates that we, as humans, still need, crave and benefit from face-to-face encounters with people . . . and food.

MORE HOSTING TIPS

Hosts see to the comfort of their guests. They can arrange to leave a credit card with the manager so that there are no financial dealings at the table. Private clubs have this advantage. Most seasoned corporate executives are well versed in the formalities and amenities of hosting meals, meetings, and parties or they wouldn't be executives and leaders. Here are some additional reminders for the host:

- Guests are seated with their backs to the banquette; hosts face their guests.
- Hosts may give the meal order for everyone but may not choose the meals unless asked to do so.
- Hosts check with the guests to see if they would like more wine, dessert, and so on.
- Remember: most aware guests do observe the leader.

Impeccable manners are an asset. Letitia Baldridge, Miss Manners, and myriad manners mavens serve up the rules. If the purpose of the meal is celebratory, calling ahead to arrange the surprise champagne or chocolate decadence mousse torte is a nice touch. Most restaurant personnel will cooperate.

The Flip(pant) Side

We should be sure that we're being as gracious, congenial, and as clear as possible with restaurant personnel. At an elegant birthday lunch, friend and former teaching colleague, Sylvia Cherezian and I observed a man hosting four women at a holiday lunch in a posh restaurant. His charm oozed in the conversation with his four female associates, and the P&C (power and control) were visible and audible. But the tone he used with the server was patronizing, at best.

"How people treat service people is a very important reflection of character," observed Syl, who reminded me that we both had good relationships with the school secretary, custodians and paraprofessionals. How we treat restaurant personnel is observed by our lunch companions and remembered. Let's make positive memories.

I repeat: how we talk to servers says volumes about us to our dining companion, who could be our next client, boss or colleague. A waitress at a local restaurant described two regulars in the lunch crowd: "They were always doing and discussing their deals. Though you'd think these rich guys knew better, they'd raise their hand and their voices to tell me to bring them coffee.

One day I went over to them and asked why they were so rude. I told them, 'If you really want good service, be nice. Try this: When you have a moment, may I have more coffee? You'll get better service.'" I don't know if these two wheeler-dealers changed, but I learned from her and repeat her words verbatim. They're magic words that show good manners and respect for people in service professions. Restaurant personnel can make your business meal a dining pleasure when you're nice to them. And they have ways to sabotage those who are rude in their face-to-face space.

When to Switch

When to segue from social conversation you have exchanged casual conversation to the business at hand is as important as how to do so. The best time to discuss business is after you have exchanged casual conversation. The meal is about building communication and rapport and getting to know each other, and is less about eating (which we still should not do simultaneously . . . nor with our elbows, cell phone, or BlackBerrys® on the table).

A wall hanging in the window of a local needlepoint shop caught my eye as I walked by it. It's a reminder of table manners for children and works for adults as well.

Table Manners

- Chew with your mouth closed.
- Put your napkin in your lap.
- Don't talk with your mouth full.
- Sit up straight.
- Don't start eating until everyone is served.
- Take small bites.
- Don't play with your food.
- Say "Please" and "Thank you."
- Keep both feet on the floor.
- Excuse yourself before leaving the table.

I've seen grown-ups who don't follow these simple rules. The rule I break is the one about both feet on the floor. At 4'11", sometimes my feet don't hit the floor, so I sit on one foot. Note to self—don't do that!

If every manager, new hire, associate and potential executive really knew manners, corporate America would not have to hire experts to train their MBAs, IT staff, CPAs, sales personnel, and so on, in the rules of etiquette. And it's a growing industry.

THE GUEST LIST OF DO'S AND DON'TS

The list of appropriate guest behaviors is long. Guests should be mindful that a hosted lunch may not be the time to order their two favorite dishes—caviar and lobster—unless the host recommends them and orders some. "What do you recommend?" is a question that gives your host the opportunity to provide some guidelines. Keep in mind that expense accounts are less prevalent and sometimes less generous these days. An East Coast account executive encountered a dinner guest who didn't think of this: "She ordered a seven-course meal at an à la carte restaurant and several rounds of liquid refreshment. I'm surprised she also didn't stick me with the Pepto Bismol bill."

Being a gracious guest includes being a good listener, as well as being conversant. We all must bring something to the "Banquet of Banter." Read the paper, listen to news talk, and come prepared with three to five items to chat about. Visit their Web site and Google your hosts to see if they have any news, have won any awards or have written a published brief. Your hosts will provide the dining guidelines. If they don't indulge in an alcoholic beverage, you may want to follow that lead.

As It Is Written . . . (So Shall It Be!)

The guest should always send a thank-you to the host, who, at the very least, provided sustenance. E-mail a quick acknowledgement, then send a handwritten note. Yes, I know it's old school to suggest sending a handwritten note and it takes time. But in this fast-paced, digital, wireless world, nothing says personal touch more than the handwritten note. People save them. Major corporations provide correspondence cards for people to use for personalization.

According to the Wall Street Journal (August 23, 2007), there has been a revival in the sales of stationery. One way to make an impression is to pick up a pen and apply it to good stationery. If everyone else is texting or e-mailing, be different and write a note! And if the host provided sustenance in the form of leads, consultation, advice, feedback, or ideas, a gift of acknowledgement is also appropriate. Remember: the gift of time is precious.

In this e-mail message era, a handwritten note has become even more personal and memorable. It indicates that you took time to take pen in hand to thank someone for the precious time he or she gave to you. Remember the impression made by the last handwritten note you received? I still have those I've received from Tom Peters and Jack Canfield and a number of students from my presentations at NYU's Summer Publishing Institute. They're special to me.

Sheryl Oberman, owner of The Stationery Station in Highland Park, Illinois, corroborates the Wall Street Journal findings. "The handwritten note is flourishing. Little else beats the discovery of a special envelope, addressed by hand. It's more appropriate to use a handwritten note after a job interview, for bridal shower and wedding thank-yous, and for any message where communication is intended to be more personal. Rather than e-mail, the personal note conveys more accurately one's message."

Today is the best time to start being a good guest. Write notes of thanks.

HOW TO AVOID A "SPLITTING" HEADACHE

There's not much that intimidates me: not an audience of one thousand, not a roomful of strangers, nor a fear of flying! But three things do cause me great discomfort:

1. Turkeys (the birds, not people) and cooking them.
2. People who wash silk while the rest of us pay $9.95 to clean it!
3. Great Divide—if the idea of involuntarily underwriting someone's caviar, lobster, and champagne when you're not the DH (designated host) annoys you, too, read on.

I have always accepted and encouraged the easier, equal division of the dinner bill. The logic is that a few dollars is not important enough to waste time and energy dividing the bill proportionately. One friend told me of dining with seven colleagues and how they democratically split the tab. It was a day she didn't feel well, so she only had an appetizer and a cup of tea. Her portion of the bill was $70! Any way you cut it, that's a lot of money for what she ate and drank. Her husband's solution was, "Order what you want to eat and drink, 'cause the others will pay for part of it." Perhaps that's a male/female dining difference.

Avoid Cheap-Skating on Thin Ice

Why do we stay quiet? Often it's that we don't want to appear cheap or to be perceived as ungracious. This happens to me often, as I don't eat or drink that much. The real question is: Am I the only person in the world who suffers from the Dutch treat dilemma? In hopes that I was not the only patsy, I decided to do an informal survey. So I called people and posed the situation to them. People were kind enough to be candid. The results corroborate my discomfort and educated me.

If you want to be a hero at a Dutch treat meal, say something to the group if you notice that a person only had soup and coffee. Often the "demi-diner" won't say anything, but if you do, you'll have a friend who'll be appreciative. Leslie Taglio, of The Taglio Company, is a friend who has that special quality. When we go to dinner and I don't have any liquid refreshment, she never lets me split her wine bill. Leslie's view: "It's just common sense and common courtesy. If you care about a person, why would you want to take advantage of them?" She finds that easy to do when there are only two or three people, but "when there's a big group, it's easier to divide the bill evenly. Just think of it as a party—the evening's entertainment."

The idea of picking up tabs or splitting checks may not be a problem for anyone on an expense account, but what about those who pay their own way, whether it's a social or business meal? People don't want to appear cheap. However, the idea of forking out seventy dollars for a salad and hot tea, no matter how delicious they are, seems very unfair. And costly.

There's another way to look at the issue. Diane K. Danielson, founder of the Downtown Women's Clubs, said she considers the split meal, regardless of what she ordered, to be a cost of doing business. This may not work for salaried workers who have more budget constraints and can't write off their meals.

Dining Sense and Dollars

A fellow speaker told me of a woman who owned a public relations firm and suggested they have lunch. "I had prearranged to pick up the tab. She spent the meal persistently trying to sell me her PR services. Then she ordered lunch to bring home to her significant other and provided no credit card or cash to cover it. So I ended up paying for the mangé a trois!" When I asked why on earth he would let himself get taken like that, his good-natured response was, "I was so stunned I couldn't say anything." But he has now . . . to others in our association as a forewarning about her freeloading tendencies.

In addition, I learned several things from my informal interviews with a number of people:

1. There is no pat solution.
2. There are different mindsets about the issue of group dining.
3. There are different observations and realities for men and women.

- Men more often are on expense accounts and expect to pick up tabs. And expense accounts are shrinking.

- Some women tend to spend more time identifying each person's total. Several women I interviewed decried the haggling they had seen. A male business associate is more understanding because, "Overall, women still earn less than men!"
- Men more often expect to split bills evenly, regardless of what they drink or eat. But nobody wants to be used.

More Chutzpah Redefined

"One time there was a group of twenty of us who went out after a meeting. One fellow drank a liqueur that cost $25 per glass and had five rounds. He managed to be on the dance floor when the bill arrived!" That fellow is a major contender for the chutzpah award. But he has lots of competition. One professional said her ire was up the evening she and five colleagues went to dinner. One of them was a self-appointed wine connoisseur who felt compelled to order a $75 bottle for everyone to share (both in sips and cents) "and most of us couldn't tell the difference between a $28 bottle and the $75 one!"

According to my informal survey, there wasn't a problem when it was clear that the person who extended the invitation was the host. The dining experience became an issue when there was no designated host.

While having dinner in San Francisco with my childhood friend, Pam Massarsky, a lobbyist for the Chicago Teachers Union, I heard another side of the issue: "My late husband David [Peterson] worked for the Chicago Teachers Union, and he loved to eat when we went out to dinner. He'd eat a full seven-course meal, have a martini, wine, and an after-dinner drink. He'd refuse to split the tab because he didn't want to feel constrained by the person who had a piece of fish with a cup of coffee. David handled this by saying up front to our dinner companions, 'You just pay for what your share is; we are not splitting the tab.' And he paid the rest."

Being up-front is the key. There are many people who do not drink. My friend Pam Martens is one of them. "When I go out with other people, I say upfront that I am happy to split the food tab, but I won't pay for alcohol. Nobody has ever complained or refused to include me at dinner."

In a recent letter to Amy Dickinson, Ann Landers's successor, a letter writer asked what she could do as a nondrinker about paying an exorbitant amount for the alcohol consumed. Short of staying home, Amy recommended that she should start standing up for herself and setting parameters before partaking (Marin Independent Journal, August 12, 2007). That works for Pam Martens as well. Most restaurants will run a separate liquor tab if asked.

A "Host" of Solutions

Some proposed solutions to the dilemma:

1. Ask whether the meal is hosted, Dutch or split: Dutch—pay your own way (this often becomes a split); split—divided evenly; hosted—tab is picked up.

   Make your decision accordingly about joining the group. Or you can join the group later for coffee. Place a five-dollar bill on the table, which should cover coffee, tax, and your share of the tip.

2. One woman I know told me that she always gives her exact amount so that she never feels ripped off. But others do if the "exact" amount is less than adequate for her share, and it usually is. Adding an extra five dollars keeps anyone from being stuck with her uncalculated extras. Barry Wishner recently got stuck paying the balance of a tab incurred at a dinner with colleagues. They paid what they thought was their share. But the wine bill was $120. "Because I was the last to leave, the waiter came to me to collect the balance. It's not that $25 will set me back, but we need a better system or a better table accountant."

   When there are shortages, the waitstaff often gets stiffed, which simply isn't fair.

3. If you're the guest, don't take advantage. Be wallet-friendly.

4. A word to those offenders who order the most expensive food and a number of drinks and costly wine: we may suffer silently at the table, but you can bet that tomorrow we're burning up the blogosphere and the wires with the word on you! The network works in mysterious ways. Take a hint from David Peterson: "Offer to pay the full amount you have incurred and throw in a little extra!"

5. Another solution is to choose restaurants that will give separate checks. This may be extra work for the server and/or restaurant, but it surely makes sense to ask. In this case, a 20 percent tip is in order.

6. As for tips, a bigger party is more work for the server. Throwing in an extra couple of dollars each for the tip will mean little to us and will mean a lot to the hardworking server.

Making the Meal Deal Real

- Breaking bread may make or break your business or career! Unless it's the dessert, there should be no BlackBerrys in sight.
- Dining know-how is a nuance of networking.
- Make it your business to avoid being a real meal schlemiel.
- ET may phone home after lunch but not during it.

ROANE'S REMINDERS

* A business meal is a quasi-social/business event necessitating a working knowledge of etiquette. Power and control plays may have their place in megameals when negotiating for megadeals. However, these P&C antics are inappropriate during a lunch, which is supposed to increase the circle of contacts, establish connections, and grow business relationships.

* Hosts have responsibilities for prearranging specifics, seeing to the comfort of guests, contributing to the flow of conversation, setting the time parameters, and picking up the tab as inconspicuously as

possible. If you're the receiver of ideas, leads, advice, or information, you're the host.

* When dining alone, it's okay to have a cell phone conversation, as long as it's quiet and unobtrusive and doesn't violate restaurant policy.

* Guests would be well advised to observe the host's behavior as a guideline for ordering food and drink.

* Prepare conversation to contribute to the flow.

* The only big-time operation that requires a cell phone at lunch is a heart transplant. Unless you're the heart surgeon or recipient, leave your phone in your pocket or purse.

* Splitting tabs may be a problem that can be prevented by prior planning and clear communication. If you don't drink and don't want to pay part of the bar bill, ask the server for a separate bar tab.

* If you view dinner with the gang as an evening meal and entertainment (if the gang is entertaining), then the cost of the meal includes the show.

* If your budget is very lean, you can decline the invitation rather than risk a dent in the pocket and a don't in the face-to-face space.

Chapter Six

Office Politics Are Here to Stay

n Evita, my favorite Andrew Lloyd Weber musical, one of the generals proclaims politics as "the art of the possible." Having a keen sense of office politics can dramatically impact your life, because it's an aspect of interpersonal communication that shows you're paying attention to the dynamics in your workplace. It's a skill that successful leaders possess. When we also have a network of contacts in other departments and colleagues in other companies, we're privy to informal information that helps shape our decisions, behavior and plans and increases the possibilities in our career.

The beauty of being in the face-to-face space is that we can observe, listen and interact in real time. People who have no desk at the corporate office or who work remotely have been known to feel left out of the mainstream, because they no longer have access to social interactions that are part of workplace communication and office politics. Although Web-based conference calls with an instant messaging component allow for interaction, it's a viable alternative but not a substitute. Politically astute remote workers allocate time to work onsite if they are able to do so, in order to stay connected with their coworkers and boss and have access to the dynamics of the workplace.

A TIMELY TIME-SAVER

Too often, people are overheard complaining about the politics of a situation as being manipulative, claiming, "I just want to do my job well." Let me share a longstanding, time-saving tip: Please don't waste one moment lamenting about the horrible politics in your office, organization, or volunteer association. There's no gathering of three or more people free of politics. Remember the last family holiday reunion you attended? Maybe you'd rather not.

Being armed with political business savvy is a critical quality that bears attention. Without it, you will lack awareness of the players, the written and the unwritten rules and policies, and the way the organization operates. If we aren't savvy, our resources may, like the water in a California drought, dry up.

POLITICAL SAVVY SECURES SUCCESS

The term politics has often conjured up an image of the cigar-chomping, deal-making, sleazy character, making many of us grow up thinking that politics is a dirty word. After my years as a public school teacher in Chicago and San Francisco, I can assure you that politics is not an invective, at least not one for which we send students to the principal's office. There's a range of cuss words now heard on cable television, in music or movies, and on playgrounds across the country, and one of those provocatively used bad words is not politics.

Many people blame office politics for loss of positions, promotions and career mobility because it's convenient to do so. We may see someone whose promotion completely baffles us. But that promotion can motivate us to secure our own promotion by taking on projects with visibility, increasing our interaction with coworkers, and opening up dialogue with superiors.

There are specific abilities and skills required of every job, but heightened political awareness of how any organization, corporation, formal or informal network operates, who operates it, and the implicit policies contributes to our effectiveness on the job. We need to know who we can go to and when we can be the go-to person on any project.

IN SEARCH OF RED TAPE CUTTERS

Growing up in Chicago, where you didn't have to be alive to vote, I learned early on that there were two kinds of people: (1) red tape cutters and (2) red tape creators. The red tape cutters would say, "It looks like we have a policy snag, but let me make a call. I have a friend whose cousin is in that department who might help." And they make the call! Red tape creators have neither the imagination nor the resources, and they're the "by-the-book" people who don't make things happen with any frequency.

Besides having a network of resources, another benefit of heightened political skill is having a grasp of how things are done and who makes things happen. Most of us want to do business with red tape cutters and, in fact, be them ourselves. What we want to hear, when we have a problem, is: "Call Joe. If he can't help you fix your problem, he knows who can." Whether you're a cop or corporate executive, having a diverse database of doers helps get the job done.

As an aside, there are still those of us in this era of contact management programs and social networking sites who also keep a Rolodex™ on our desk. The Wall Street Journal (November 24, 2007) highlighted top executives who are still using their rotary card catalogs to file and find their contacts. They never have to worry about a computer glitch or power outage destroying their database. The important point is not which method of contact management we use but how we manage our contact with those we know.

OFFICE IMPOLITICS

The person's professional drawback of not being aware of office and organizational politics show in a person's lack of ability to get things done and the perception that he or she can't accomplish the necessary goals.

The Five Fatal Flaws of Floundering at Office Politics

The possible perceptions could be that a person is:

1. Missing a critical skill.
2. Lacking awareness.
3. Not being a team player or does not have a network of sources and resources.
4. Lacking in common sense. This umbrella term has come to encompass logic, practicality, savvy and know-how.
5. Untrustworthy with confidences and critical information.

KNOW THE ABCS

We need to know who's on our A team, the people whom we can call on and trust without equivocation. Then there's the B team. They're the people with whom there's some connection and communication that's positive and pleasant. And the C team has the people we'd rather not C (see). They're not in our corner—never will be—and are potential saboteurs. Know thine enemy and keep him or her close. Large corporations have larger numbers of these players, but every office, family and volunteer organization has them, too. It just is.

A recent Harvard Business Review article (November 2007) identified the perennial problem solver. While the ability to resolve conflicts and problems is valued, some of the solvers are the cause of the conflicts they resolve. Reading this reminded me of a conversation I had with a member of the local school board about another board member. "Of course, she's able to solve the conflicts and problems. After all, she started them."

Nathan Bennet of Georgia Tech's College of Management calls it "Munchausen at Work Syndrome." Munchausen Syndrome is a psychological disorder where the person fabricates symptoms and diseases to get attention. Munchausen at work may not be common, but the person who is putting out too many office fires may well be the person starting them and is someone to be avoided.

QUICK QUIZ

Following is a quick quiz (self-administered, of course) to determine whether you have a sense of office politics.

Do events occur that continually surprise you? If your answer is yes, that can be remedied. The face-to-face space provides an opportunity to develop the crucial awareness of your workplace. Here are some actions you can take:

- Observe your colleagues, subordinates and supervisors. Who eats with whom? Works out together? Commutes together?
- Read the body language of your coworkers as names, projects and assignments are mentioned.
- Listen to conversations in the elevators, staff rooms, nearby restaurants and even the washrooms.
- Converse with your coworkers, clients, colleagues and competitors.
- Join company groups and teams. Volunteer for community projects.

POLITICALLY PROACTIVE

According to Samuel Bacharch, professor at Cornell University and author of Get Them On Your Side (Fast Company, New York, May 2005, p. 13), having political competence is a skill you learn. It's the difference between who "can get an idea off the ground and who can't." When we have awareness of the interpersonal dynamics of office politics, our communication and collaboration becomes more finely tuned. Thus we create an opportunity to persuade folks and build coalitions. And more gets done! The "art of the possible" is in place.

DON'T GET WRITTEN OFF

Our written communication demonstrates whether we have office political smarts. We need to be sure that memos and e-mails are answered and appropriate, and favors of every flavor are acknowledged. These e-mails and memos must be written clearly, carefully, concisely, and with correct English. As with any written document, they must reflect well on the writer.

Hot Tip

After the memo is drafted, give it the sixty-minute test. Reread it an hour later to be sure it conveys the information, tone and call to action that accomplish the task.

RECIPROCITY RULES

There's another critical career tool that fits under the umbrella of office politics that operates in our workplace and our personal space. When reciprocity exists, it's viewed as awareness coupled with positive action. When it's missing, a career can be damaged by a perceived lack of know-how.

Reciprocity is a cornerstone of life. It's a common courtesy, the give and take that's the glue that sticks things together. Giving, without expectation, works. But not giving back, definitely does not.

I learned early on (Chicago style) that reciprocity is a very basic behavior. It's crucial to business careers and personal lives. I've heard tales of unsavory, impolitic people who never acknowledge what they receive—time, advice, clients, contacts, leads or gifts—let alone, trade back. It's as if the me-generation mentality permeated and devastated the area once known as basic common sense. But a more solid mindset is catching on. We need to think of reciprocity as a basic courtesy as well as a critical career skill. If we choose not to value, acknowledge and return kindness and

favors when possible, we must be prepared to suffer the consequences.

There's a school of networking that's calculated to cajole people into giving to get back. But that's mired in self-interest and
can backfire. Once again, if we have time to receive help, favors,
gifts or advice, we're wise to take the time to give acknowledgement as well as return the boon, which is a common courtesy. If
not, our sources of support could dry up. People talk, the word
gets out, and writers and bloggers get great material.

Being known to be a person of character is the ultimate intrinsic reward. In a nutshell, one good turn does indeed deserve
another.

MANAGING THE "MARKERS"

I believe it's possible to have two different schools of thought on
the same issue at the same time: a yin and yang. On the one hand,
we need to give, share and support without strings (yin). On the
other hand, the politics of life indicate we need to be cognizant
about whom and what we owe because of what was done for us
(yang).

There are times when I feel that I'm in a scene from one of
my all-time favorite movies, Guys & Dolls. No, I'm not Miss Ad-
elaide, the chorus girl, nor Sister Sarah, the Salvation Army angel.
I hear myself sounding like Big Jule, the boss of the Chicago
organization, explaining that Sky Masterson is "holding my markers." In the movie, these markers were a gambling debt paid up
by attending a Salvation Army meeting. But Big Jule knew that he
took the gamble, played the game, and lost . . . and that he now
owed Sky Masterson. It's simple, the clear-cut rules of the game.
Play, Lose, Owe.

Working in the business world, having a career, growing a
business, or entering a profession is also a gamble. You enter the
game; there are stakes (and much at stake); you learn the rules
and the culture; you're dealt a hand. Play your cards right, work

hard and well, and your business gains. You move up the career ladder, and your professional expertise and status increase.

In our personal and professional lives, we do favors for people in myriad situations because they need our help and we're willing to give it. When we need support, assistance or information, letting those people we've helped know we need help makes sense. If you've assisted them, why wouldn't they want to return the support? We need to ask, or at the very least, let people know what we need. The politically wise person reciprocates, as does the good friend.

If we don't do favors and help people, that could be an unwise choice. The lesson was reinforced in an episode of Grey's Anatomy where the plastic surgeon (Dr. Sloan) wanted to perform pro bono surgery on a young boy to reconstruct his ears. He tells Dr. Grey, "I have no social capital. I can't get any of the staff to do me a favor, because I've never done favors for any of them." Case closed.

There are reasons people refrain from asking for help. According to Psychology Today (September/October 2007, p. 16), asking for help challenges a person's self-esteem. Those who can offer assistance may have to go out of their way to give it to those who need it because those in need may not admit it. An investment in social capital is savvy as well as kind.

HEDGING OUR BETS

We all want to hedge our bets in the game of life. One way to do so is to listen to Big Jule. Our network will stop supporting us if we don't pay back. We need to be politically astute, to know what chits (favors) are out there, who holds our markers (and for what), and whose markers are in our possession. Our position in our business, profession, and social circle depends on it. Sometimes we call in the favor, not for ourselves, but to help a friend, relative or colleague. Reciprocity is not tit for tat because we often choose designated receivers.

Savvy people know and understand that politics permeate the group in every phase of life: education, charity organizations, medicine, business, religion. It's not a sad commentary or a negative one; it's a realistic one.

We shouldn't waste a moment whining or worrying about the presence of politics; instead, we need to be mindful of it. Savvy people who are politically astute know the score. We can all name people who don't know the score; they just don't get it. As a friend so aptly put it, "They're the clue-impaired."

FAVOR-ITISM

Some people are uncomfortable with recognizing that they've been given help or favors. Others are undone by the thought of asking for help, let alone calling in old favors. The reality is that we must allow people to return the favors we have done for them in the office and in our personal lives for several reasons:

1. It relieves people of the pressure and guilt of owing us.
2. It gives people an opportunity to give, which clears the slate, so then they feel they've been helpful and have reciprocated.
3. And we continue to give the help, advice, and contacts that others need, as well as to be the recipients. The politically astute understand the benefit of allowing others to return their help.

One of my friends has a longtime friend who is very wealthy. "He always wants to pick up the tab for our dinners because he knows it's easier for him to do so." But my friend is smart. "Every so often I grab the check, because I want to treat him, and he understands I can't always be the guest."

THE BALANCING ACT—HIGHLY WIRED

Whether you work in an office or are an entrepreneur who deals with clients, associates or vendors, favors are part of politics and are tricky, as they can tacitly obligate the recipient. The grantor also has to be careful in how he or she grants the favor and must give, or even create, an opportunity for payback.

I know some people who are superb at getting favors; they even make the giver feel fortunate to grant the goody. Once we identify this manipulative modus operandi, most of us tend to move away and for good reason: no one wants to feel used. We walk highly wired tightropes, and the fall from grace—and high wire—has repercussions.

Hot Tip

We need to ask people to assist us in ways that they may comfortably do so. To ask people for something they cannot deliver can cause a strain. We need to be givers and receivers, and that's the beauty of balance.

THE BACKSTABBERS

Backstabbers exist in every group. In fact, the legendary O'Jays immortalized them in song. "They smile in your face and all the time they want to take your place . . . the backstabbers." They're the insecure, the jealous, and even the entitled, who concoct plans of sabotage that they implement fearlessly.

Dr. Judith Briles, in her groundbreaking book, Woman to Woman 2000: Becoming Sabotage Savvy in the New Millennium (New Horizon Press, Far Hills, New Jersey, 2000), suggests that we directly confront those who are perpetrating these problems. "Doing so gets the issue out in the open." It's best to do so tactfully, choosing your words carefully, but not allowing the backstabber to get away with the sabotage. Being called on it will often stop the behavior. But saying nothing gives an implicit, silent approval.

When we've identified allies and supporters, are known in our professional associations, have relationships with coworkers who are on every rung of the corporate ladder, work hard and smart, observe the interpersonal interactions in our workplace and are nice to people, our sense of office politics becomes finely honed. That allows us to do our jobs, collaborate and contribute to the overall success of the organization. We're then known for being "in the know," and that's a prime position.

ROANE'S REMINDERS

* Office politics is merely a process. It's present in every phase and relationship of life, and we should accept it and increase our awareness of it.
* Use your time in the face-to-face space to observe and gain insights.
* Build social capital by helping others in areas and ways they need assistance.
* Reciprocity rules, because giving and taking are to be done in balance.
* Become a red tape cutter by building a network of sources and resources.
* Manage your markers: know who you owe and who owes you, and who you can ask for support, ideas, and favors.
* Call in your favors, not just for yourself but for others or for charity, in order to clear the slate.
* Pay back favors without being asked. Politically savvy people reciprocate without requests.

Chapter Seven

Facing the Phone Fear Factor

The simple truth is that the telephone, whether it's a land line, cell phone, or computer-based call, is an intrinsic part of the fabric of business and personal life. Thus we must mind our phone manners and our manner of using the phone. Though there are people in our business and personal lives who prefer to communicate digitally, the ability, willingness and interest to communicate by telephone continues to be a valuable personal and professional skill. When Intel instituted its "zero e-mail Friday's" in favor of "get up and talk to the person in the next cubicle," the directive also emphasized using the phone to enhance communication.

This chapter is about using the telephone to stay in touch, to follow up and to be connected. In this brave new digital world, there are people who avoid the use of the phone. Some claim it takes up too much time. Others avoid the phone because they may be shy or are uncomfortable with messages that can't be edited. In order to reclaim and retain your personal touch, I would encourage you to include the phone as part of your staying-in-touch options for conducting business communication.

THE ATTITUDE PLATITUDE

Although today a growing number of people have no land-line phone, I have always believed that my attachment to the source of nourishment in life was a telephone cord, not the umbilical cord!

It may be that my positive attitude has permitted me to make the phone my friend . . . and to be a phone friend. Research continues to show that people who have relaxed phone conversations with friends are happier and healthier. And that's good news.

Today's economy and lifestyle require us to be effective, efficient and connected, and at the same time we must also communicate and build rapport. Telephone conversations help us meet those requirements when a face-to-face meeting or get-together is not possible.

Our advanced technology has changed and enhanced what was once a basic avenue of communication. People can now call from their cars, while walking down a street, in an elevator, from the bathroom (please don't do that), and from the bleachers at a baseball game. Some phones are built into cars. There are digital phones, and, Lord, have mercy, videophones. It isn't enough that the phone could be intrusive; now we have to look good if we're interrupted! This is a frightening thought, although not a new one. The Chicago Museum of Science and Industry had an AT&T picture phone exhibit over forty years ago.

There was a time that hero Dick Tracy's ability to talk to his watch was a comic book fantasy. And Maxwell Smart (Agent 88, Don Adams) making spy calls on the phone in his shoe in the '70s was goofy fun. It still is, as Steve Carrell, the current Maxwell Smart, phones in through his loafer.

NEWS WITH CUES

When a face-to-face meeting is impossible, the next best option is a phone conversation. It's also two-way and you get to hear tone, inflection and intent. Some people choose to avoid using the phone in favor of e-mails, text messaging and instant messages, but these modes of messaging are cue-less. There's no question that each of these technologies contributes to communication and helps us stay connected. But there's something to be said for speaking with people rather than at them. Something unplanned and wonderful could happen as the conversation moves organically from subject to subject.

THE "SHORT" ANSWER

Most of us have stories of trying to reach a person when we have a problem that needs to be solved with a product or service, as we have ended up spending time in computer voice-generated "voice jail." Ironically, the outbound greeting is often, "Your phone call is important to us!" Really? You've got to be kidding! We end up talking to these computer-generated voices, pressing buttons on the dial pad and trying to override the phone system to get a real person to solve our concerns. Having to endure that irritating process inherently says, "Your phone call means not a whit to us."

John "Shorty" Sneed is president of the Mississippi division of one of the top 100 insurance agencies in the country. Headquartered in Gulfport, Mississippi, Shorty has 175 employees in several offices. "I find those computer phone systems to be irritating and customer-unfriendly, so I'm not going to annoy my clients with one. We have a human being who answers our phones and warmly greets our customers. Her tone of voice is friendly yet businesslike. Her salary is not an expense; it's an investment."

Shorty hit upon an important point. Any client of his agency is greeted warmly. With a couple of seasons of The Office (both the British and U.S. versions) under our belts, we've seen and heard how Pam, the receptionist, does it from Scranton, Pennsylvania. Being warm, friendly, and efficient is the Trifecta of phone traits.

Everything old is new again. Even Netflix has made the decision that, in order to compete, it would do something different: have real people answer its customer service calls. Imagine that! What a brilliantly analog, personal touch. The company's call center, according to the New York Times (August 4, 2007), is in the Portland, Oregon, area. Michael Osier, vice president for information technology operations, picked the greater Portland area because of the genial attitude of the residents. "Based on research for phone-based customer service of Southwest Airlines and American Express, customers preferred human interaction over e-mail messages." That makes sense to me.

REGIONAL DIFFERENCES

We'd like to think that all regions of the country operate on the same principles, but that simply isn't true. More than one audience member, colleague and friend have said that there's a distinct difference between an East Coast phone call and one from the South, or from the Midwest, or from the West Coast.

CPA, Lana Teplick, lived and worked in Boston for over three decades. "There's a noticeable difference between Boston, Massachusetts, and Mobile, Alabama, where I now live. Back East, when I made a client call, I said my name, 'How are you?' and got to the point of the business call. Maybe we'd chat briefly after the business at hand. Not so in Mobile. I say my name, ask people how they are, listen to the answer, then ask about their kids, they inquire about my daughter, Alexis, I fill them in, and then we get to the business at hand. It's a different phone style and illustrates that we have to be cognizant of and adapt to regional communication differences." Again, we need to hear and take our cues from the other person's voice.

THE REVOLT AGAINST THE REVOLUTION

The telephone revolutionized communication, and now, more than a century later, has precipitated a new revolt. Because of telemarketing, the phone, a once highly valued invention, is being viewed with suspicion when it rings. Many of us pay for caller ID so that we know when to avoid the call. Yet the telephone remains a tool that keeps us connected to clients, colleagues, family, and friends. Although we send cards, e-mails, text messages and notes (an endangered species of communication), when face-to-face conversations are impossible, the phone is the best interactive technological tool. Again, it affords us the opportunity to learn by hearing another's conversational style, to intuit the emotions and to respond appropriately. We "reach out and touch someone."

According to author/humorist Fran Liebowitz, there's an additional bonus: "The telephone is a good way to talk to people without having to offer them a drink."

MANAGING MOMENTS AND MINUTIA

The beauty of the telephone is that it's a two-way (or more) means of communication. But for some of us, the interactive nature of the phone is its biggest liability. In an era where work goes on 24/7, "managing moments" is valued as a time-saving tip for ultimate career success, and participating in an actual conversation is considered time-consuming or uncomfortable. Why? There are a half dozen possible reasons:

1. Some people find they're too busy to take time on the phone. After all, someone may take sixty-two seconds sharing a response!

2. Some people don't consider themselves good on the phone, so they choose not to struggle.

3. Some people fear rejection. "I used to be so very intimidated by the phone, fearing possible rejection," revealed Ruthe Hirsch, producer of the musical Day at the Bay. "I observed a colleague place phone calls with ease; he was having a good time talking with people. I followed his example. Now, instead of thinking of them as contacts, I enjoy speaking with them as people."

4. Some people are more comfortable with written methods of communicating where they can edit and plan their words.

5. People stay away from phones because they're shy.

6. Last, but not least, the phone call can be intrusive—both at work and at home. Many people are respectful of that possibility. They would rather use e-mail to set a time to talk that is mutually convenient.

Growing up in my house, if the phone rang after 10:00 P.M., my parents assumed it could only be bad news, and it usually was.

There are times when sending e-mails or text messages makes more sense. They deliver a bit of information concisely ("the meeting was changed to 2:30 P.M.," "the order is confirmed," "are you in town next week?") in a timely manner. While other people are managing their moments by avoiding the phone, dare to be different.

> **Hot Tip**
>
> Be memorable. Pick up the phone; spend a moment making small talk. Invest a minute or two in having conversation that builds a connection.

Companies that are trying to cut down on the deluge of e-mails in their inboxes have another goal: to encourage face-to-face interaction and phone conversation because both are integral to business.

The risk: you'll lose a few minutes. Big deal! The rewards: you'll increase your connections, network, resources, information base, and power. You'll build rapport. Maybe you'll find a tennis partner, a job lead, a fellow video game enthusiast, or even . . . a friend!

THE PHONE AS PROBLEM SOLVER

Most of us have encountered the misfired, misread, miserable effects of the misinterpreted e-mail exchange. The tone of what Jim has written and its intent are not heard when John reads the e-mail.

When I spoke to the Navy, Captain Joseph Horn, Jr., told me he had two newer engineers working together. "They cc'd me on a volley of e-mail exchanges. I finally got up from my desk to find them and they were sitting almost next to each other. Instead of a verbal face-to-face conversation, they chose to use e-mail, which wasted their time, my time and escalated the problem."

Hot Tip

Some people say that if the volley is more than three rounds, pick up the phone. But there's a better barometer. If you're taking more than five minutes to compose an e-mail, use the phone. A two-way conversation is the way two can solve issues twice as fast. And there's no paper trail!

CUT TO THE CHASE

We need to be up front about our calls. Mark Chimsky, editor-in-chief of Sellers Publishing, Inc., is so friendly and personable that we became phone friends a year before we met face to face. He recalled a conversation that was not quite what it initially seemed to be. "A former colleague of mine called and spent fifteen minutes schmoozing (engaging in easygoing discussion). It was okay, as I thought it was simply a friendly catch-up call. Then he asked for a big favor. I resented the fact that he called with a specific agenda in mind but led me to believe that it was just a casual call. I would've preferred it if he had been much more direct and asked his favor two minutes into the conversation. My advice in such circumstances: Cut to the chase. Start out with a few pleasantries. Be genuinely interested. If you're requesting a favor, make sure you're open and up front about it and be respectful of the other person's time—always. It will be appreciated." Mark, good-natured as he is, felt he was misled and used.

IN "MANNERS" OF SPEAKING

When the original San Francisco Examiner featured a weekly "Careers" column, I was the consulting coordinator and a frequent contributor. The business editor referred queries from interested writers to me. One of these people, now a professional speaker, had met me through mutual acquaintances and decided to befriend me in order to write for the series. Her ploy was "Let me share my vast resources with you, and you can do the same." Because she wanted to get her byline in the newspaper, she called several times. Each time I stopped what I was doing and pleasantly responded. She then stopped me in midsentence and clearly (more or less, adamantly) said, "Susan, that is not on my agenda." Whoa! Her agenda? In case you're wondering, she never did get to write any columns for the career series. After her phone faux pas, it just wasn't "on my agenda."

It makes sense to have a few notes prepared before you call. But these notes are merely memory joggers, not cast-in-concrete scripts that prohibit others from having their say. Some would consider this Communications/Political Deal Maker a terrific time manager, but not I. She forgot that her agenda had nothing to do with me. She neglected to remember that her calls interrupted me, and she didn't value my time. Consequently, she didn't manage her manners. The irony is that she's on the speaking circuit teaching others to do the same.

All people are busy with the demands of job, community, and professional organizations, as well as personal and family life. What will distinguish us is how we handle that busyness.

THE MENACE OF MULTITASKING

Kerry Davis, owner of the Word Weaver Secretarial Service, said that she called to hire a subcontractor who had submitted a proposal for a project. As they spoke, "I heard the sound of her computer keys clicking away. Her message was clear, 'My inputting is more important than your comments about the project.' It was so discourteous I decided to hire someone else."

Although women have been multitasking for years, both men and women now pride themselves on doing several things at once.

Current research indicates we're doing several things but rarely doing them all well! Some people can do two things at once, but few make you feel that they're paying attention to you while they're doing double duty. According to Davis, who is the patient translator of hieroglyphics of two of my books, "That includes people who eat and chew gum while talking on the phone. The message is 'I only have time to eat . . . in your ear.'" This behavior gives new meaning to the idiom, "He chewed my ear off."

Hot Tip
The wing and cracking gum while on a business phone call. You may want to do the same on personal calls.

Davis also suggests that if another person comes into your office with a question while you are on the phone with someone, don't talk to both people at once. Avoid having one of those whispered conversations on the side with one person while the other person thinks he has your full attention—until he hears that whispered conversation you're having and then feels the loss of your attention. Excuse yourself to the caller for just a moment, handle the urgent interruption (only if it's urgent; otherwise, no one should have been rude enough to bother you when you were so obviously busy with a phone call), and then return to the phone conversation.

This is tough for parents, because children seem to think that as soon as a phone is in mom's or dad's hand, the need for attention begins. One dear friend felt that it was okay for her to have a side conversation (or reprimand) with one or all of her children while I was on the line. After a number of interruptions, I tried to be sensitive and said, "I can hear you're busy. We'll talk later."

Telephone interruptions are not only made by young children. My uncle would go to Chicago to visit my mother, his older sister. When I would call to talk to her, he would start to talk to her in the middle of our conversation and she would answer him! It was frustrating. Sometimes I'd say to my mother, "I called to talk to you because I wanted to hear how you are." "So sorry, you're right, dear," would sweetly and apologetically flow from my mother's mouth. On the very next phone call, it would happen again. She couldn't stop her brother from interrupting her long-distance conversations, and she couldn't stop herself from answering him . . . while talking to me. My mother taught me a valuable lesson: If you can't give attention to the person on the phone, don't answer it. Return the call at your own convenience.

BE A PHONE FRIEND

After you've worked rooms, had face-to-face conversations, and exchanged cards, the follow-up is essential. If part of your follow-up process is a phone call, it's now a warm call to someone you know rather than a cold call to a stranger. It's even better to have a smile in your voice when placing or answering calls.

Rule: There is no way to turn a contact made at a meeting, party, or event into a connection without follow-up.

An e-mail or a text message is a good way to touch base, yet it is one-way communication. For example: You attended a committee meeting at a local community organization, meeting the other members, listening to their ideas and watching them interact. Perhaps one or two people stand out because of their ideas, delivery and demeanor. You have several options:

1. Do nothing, but that has no rewards.
2. Send an e-mail, a text message or a handwritten note expressing your positive reaction.
3. Pick up a phone: even if you have to leave a message on an answering machine or voice mail, your sincerity, warmth and acknowledgement can be heard and felt!

MAKE HAY CALLS

Staying in touch when nothing is needed is the hallmark of the savvy networker. Farrell Chiles, a former chairman of the board of BIG (Blacks in Government), has always called just to say hello. "How else do you keep connected to people if you never talk to them?" he asked rhetorically. Farrell e-mails, but he's savvy leader who stays in touch with his circle by making "How are you?" (HAY) calls as well. "Staying in touch with people just to say hello makes it easier to call when I need help with an issue." He has a cross-country collection of friends, colleagues and associates who are always happy to hear from him.

A STRANGER CALLS

One day I received a call from Charles Amico, a stranger who identified himself and the colleague who suggested he call me when he moved to San Francisco. He was full of vitality and spirit on the phone. We chatted about our mutual acquaintance, Charles's move, and San Francisco. As I hadn't been apprised, his call was unexpected and turned out to be an unexpected pleasure. We stayed in touch, met over coffee, and became buddies. We had matching energy levels, similar pacing, tone, listening skills, and laughter levels. Charlie was the original executive coach before that was a profession with certification.

I recently bumped into him and his mother, visiting from the East Coast, at the local supermarket. Mama was shopping so that she could cook some of Charlie's favorites. I looked in her basket and said, "The spinach will make you strong." Mrs. Amico looked at me, rather pityingly, and said very conclusively, "That isn't spinach. It's basil. Obviously, you aren't Italian!" It was and I'm not! I walked away smiling (and wanting to taste Mama's menu).

EFFECTIVE PHONE LINES

Charlie did it the right way. When calling at the behest of another person, for starters:

1. Identify yourself.
2. Name the person whom you are calling.
3. State the name of the connection.

"Hello, may I please speak to Jane Jones? This is Sarah Bernhardt. Eric Cartman suggested that I call," is one way to make that connection early on.

If you're in the midst of a project and the phone rings, it's acceptable to say so and excuse yourself rather than remain on the phone not conversing or doing the uh huh's. Then return the call when you said you would. If an assistant is involved in connecting your call, be sure to thank that person for his or her part. If you do reach Jane, introduce yourself with energy and a smile in your voice.

Always ask this question: "Is this a good time? If not now, when would be a better time?" If Jane has only two minutes, promise brevity and deliver it. Convey the positive comments your mutual contact has said about Jane: "Eric said you're most knowledgeable about book publishing." It's the truth and it's about her, so it could help make Jane feel more at ease and receptive. Write a follow-up e-mail to Jane acknowledging the time and information shared. And, a note to Eric!

When someone you trust suggests you ought to call someone she knows, do it. A colleague told me that I must talk to Arlynn Greenbaum, owner of Authors Unlimited. Another acquaintance said the same about author Robert Spector. They were each told the same thing about me. What started with phone calls between strangers who had a mutual acquaintance has grown into cherished friendships.

> **Hot Tip**
> Knowledgeable networkers acknowledge! Apprise everyone involved of the progress of the connection.

TO THINE OWN SELF

Communication experts conclude that similarities create the basis for the comfort that contributes to rapport. There are people who advocate mirroring other people to create rapport. I'm uncomfortable with the concept when it's taken to the extreme, as it can feel as if you're being mocked. The statement that comes to mind is "To thine own self be true." It makes sense to listen and to pay attention to tone, pacing, inflection and energy; but don't be a mimic—be yourself. After all, you're the person with whom your phone contacts will have to interact. In the long run, it's easiest to be yourself, and it saves time. You'll never have to remember to be anyone else.

THE GATEKEEPERS

The concept of getting past The Gate Keeper is taught at any number of seminars as the key to the magic kingdom. Be aware that secretaries and assistants work with their bosses, and they have an established routine for screening and placing calls. Being short, insistent or too slick with the secretary rarely has a payoff. You may get through now, but you may lose the connection long term. As Carl LaMell advises, "Remember, the assistant and the boss are a team." As an aside, Carl was named by Winning Workplaces as one of the best bosses in the Chicago area in 2006.

Pleasant, considerate communication with the secretary or assistant can only reflect positively on you. If Mr. Lane indicates that Thursday would be better, you could offer to call at a convenient time on Thursday. Then do so. You say to the assistant: "I'm

Sarah Parker. Mr. Lane is expecting my call. We met last week at a fund-raiser for the American Cancer Society." Be sure to give enough information to help Mr. Lane remember you.

> **Hot Tip**
>
> Don't use the name of a person to make a contact unless you have permission to do so.

THINK LONG TERM

As an author, I've worked with editors and their assistants on my books. It would've been foolish for me to have connived my way past the assistants. Often they were more than helpful. And they "grow up" to be executive editors, even literary agents. It wouldn't have served me to have been anything less than friendly, respectful and nice when I spoke with them on the phone.

Unless the conversation is about a serious issue, try to be lighthearted when calling, because most other people aren't. Use a mirror to make sure there's a smile on your face, and it will transfer to your voice. Pay attention to the voice on the other end. Is there stress or urgency? Ask if this is a good time; if the answer is "yes," then proceed.

How do you know where to draw the line so that a friendly phone call doesn't become too friendly? Listen. Pay attention to the cues, pauses, pace tone, paper shuffling or keyboard clicking so that you'll be mindful of people's time.

TELEPHONE TERMINATOR

If starting phone conversations is not easy, ending them may be tougher. One memorable phone call closer was from my grandmother, an immigrant whose imperfect English was her second language. When she was ready to get off the phone, she did! In her warmest grandmotherly tone, she'd say, "Thank you so much for calling." Click. She hung up. That was that! (But she made a chopped liver that more than redeemed her chopped-off conversation!)

Miss Manners suggests that the originator of the call is supposed to end it, but, "If the limits of human endurance are reached, the recipient may end it. One terminates a call by changing to a hearty voice and saying, 'Well, good,' followed by a summary, 'I'm glad to hear you closed the deal,' or, 'See you Friday.' Then, 'Take care/Aloha/Have a good weekend,' whatever makes sense. And if it was good to talk to someone, say so."

Rhymes King.

Rhymes with Orange (105945), © Hillary Price, King Features Syndicate.

YOU "AUTO" GIVE US A CALL

Cell phones really can be a blessing. I read about a Friday afternoon outdoor wedding in Tel Aviv that almost didn't take place. Sundown was fast approaching and the rabbi was late. One of the guests called a friend, the Chief Rabbi of a nearby town, who empowered a guest to conduct the ceremony via cell phone. The scene does activate the imagination. If the cell phone had had call waiting, I wonder if the bride and groom would have been left "call waiting" at the altar.

Cell phones are a time-saver and a lifesaver. But they, too, must be used appropriately. Very important calls that require excellent conditions for clarity may be ill suited for a cell phone, which may drop calls in certain areas. Although technology continues to improve, the transmission of a call as the car enters a tunnel does not! I know this firsthand, as the Waldo Grade (north of the Golden Gate Bridge) has ended many of my calls! You would hate to be in the midst of the important deal-clinching exchange only to have the line go dead . . . and maybe the deal with it. Drive time is a good time to make calls as long as both hands are on the wheel (a law in many states), driving conditions are heeded and conversations are not heated.

BACK TO BASICS

It's worth rethinking the issues of manners and etiquette as we use the tools and toys of technology. The basic questions remain: Is it courteous? Is it considerate? Is this how we should behave in shared space?

It is also important to be aware of the implicit messages we give. Does our behavior reflect respect for the other person? Or the opposite?

A Familiar Ring . . . Tone

There are many horror stories of people who attended plays, movies, memorial services, operas and dined in the better restaurants only to have the event interrupted by cell phones playing a mélange of melodies. Is that showing respect or showing off? One way to make others feel important while in our company is to turn off the cell phone. It's a way of saying, "Hold my calls. I'm with someone important." How flattering is that?

I first wrote about the cell phone phenomenon in 1992 in The Secrets of Savvy Networking. Over two decades later, cell phone rage is all the rage. Some U.S. Postal Service offices have "No Cell Phone" signs as do many restaurants. Hospitals and medical offices forbid their use. Health club locker rooms have no-cell-phone rules because of the cacophony and the cameras! And, yet, people flaunt the rules of courtesy in shared space.

The Quiet Commute

The ferry system in Marin provides for no-cell-phone areas. There are commuters who need and like the quiet. Amtrak's Acela train has a quiet car. Not only is the use of cell phones prohibited, so is loud talking. If people want to use their cell phone and have lively (loud) conversations, there are many other cars from which to choose. Observing the posted signage is a good practice and policy in all aspects of life.

Hot Tip

Living and working in shared space with some grace means that we honor the signs and requests along our pathways:

1. No cell phones.
2. Leash law in effect.
3. Handicapped parking only.
4. Reform grocery carts.
5. Rules of the Road, even if you're riding a bicycle.

Jam Sessions

The use and misuse of cell phones in public space has given us cell phone rage and a new industry. Although illegal, people are buying devices that block cell signals. The devices start at $50 and may cost more, but the fine from the FCC is about $1,000—and well worth it to those who are tired of and irritated by the incessant yammering. I predict there will be a run on these devices should the FAA ever allow cell phones on airplanes. In fact, if that comes to pass, there won't be enough sky marshals to stem the tide of "plane ole" phone rage.

The Wonders of Call Waiting

When call waiting eliminated the busy signal, this was a boon for entrepreneurs with small businesses without a full-time secretary. However, the frustration of hearing a busy signal was replaced with the frustration of deciding which call was more important: the client or the call from cousin Willie the Welcher? Mother or mother-in-law? There are times when people who have several phone lines will say, "I have a long-distance call from Tokyo that I must take." It makes sense, and no offense is taken. Call waiting operates the same way.

If that's not possible, and if a conversation is urgent and should not be interrupted, disconnect call waiting before you call. We can also disconnect incoming calls from call waiting. I do that whenever I am being interviewed on the radio. I ask producers if they would mind if I take a moment to disconnect call waiting. Not only don't they mind, they're pleased. Because of the many radio interviews that I give, this feature has been invaluable.

Radio Rude

Again, some people are so hooked to their phones that they do strange things. Author and speaker, Judith Briles, was conducting a live remote radio interview with a very animated and interesting guest. "In the middle of our live interview, we heard her call waiting signal. I was stunned when she actually put me and our live interview on hold to take the other call! After the show, I apprised her of the inappropriateness of her decision." We're not sure whether this is a sign of rudeness, chutzpah or downright ignorance.

The Return of the Phone Call

Prioritize calls, pick a good time to make and return calls, have materials prepared that you might need and pick up the phone. Do it in as timely a fashion as possible.

It makes headlines when corporate executives answer the phone, place their own calls and return calls within twenty-four hours. When I was trying to get the legendary coach, Bill Walsh, to endorse The Secrets of Savvy Networking, I called his office at Stanford Athletic Department. While I had some notes ready in case I would need to leave a message, Coach Walsh surprised me. He answered his own phone and I was tongue-tied. Finally, I sputtered that while it was an honor to speak to him, I was caught off guard. Coach Walsh could not have been nicer. He laughed and said, "Don't worry. Why don't you call my assistant in an hour?" Whew! I did. And he endorsed my book.

Hot Tip
Be prepared, just in case the person you're calling actually answers the phone!

CONFIRMING CONNECTIONS USING THE VOICE-MAIL MESSAGE: FABULOUS FOLLOW-UP

Melinda Henning, San Francisco–based speaking coach and creator of "Doing Business by Phone" training, has shared the following tips for confirming connections using voice-mail or answering machine messages.

1. The beep indicates that you now have your contact's attention and the chance to make an impact with your message.
2. Call as soon as possible after the meeting to leave a message, just as you might follow up with an e-mail in a timely manner.
3. Always leave a message. Don't waste the call. Always include the reason for the call (and a reason to return it, if you want a return call), and always leave your phone number. [Please say it slowly and clearly.]

4. Organize your message like a voice memo, announcing its contents or purpose first, and be concise. The person calling in for messages will appreciate your brevity.
5. Try something different. Be spontaneous and entertaining. Yours will be the only voice-mail message your contact gets that day that isn't boring and that makes it a standout.
6. Don't worry about mistakes. They make you sound real. Don't be afraid to laugh at yourself.
7. On your voice-mail, record a greeting in your own voice that is brief and current. If there is a number (#) or star (*) sign option to cut the message, let callers know, and when a call back might be expected. Encourage callers to leave a detailed message and tell them how long they have to talk.
8. Polish your vocal image as well as your visual image. Start smiling before you pick up the phone. To inject some energy, stand up, gesture, look in a mirror, and adopt an attitude of fun.

To leave a voice-mail message that's personable, be prepared, light and brief. Give some piece of information that will make your call different, convey energy, and give the recipient something to talk about when the call is returned. Because so few voice mails are positive, your call will stand out. Whether as a message or in person, these are the kinds of phone introductions that give people a hook on which to hang their conversation:

- "Hello. This is Arleen Honda from foggy San Francisco."
- "Hello. This is Carla Elkins from sunny Marin County."
- "Hello. This is Peter Skov from 49er country."

And be sure to say your name clearly and spell it, and repeat your number . . . slowly. And avoid leaving the way-too-long voice novel.

> **Hot Tip**
>
> If you call at an odd hour to avoid talking to a person, should he or she pick up, it's best to say, "I wanted to just leave you a message, but I'm glad you're there."

Several people have mentioned that they heard the telephone ring, picked it up, and the caller said, "I didn't expect to get you," sounding disappointed. Trust me; such a comment doesn't contribute to a connected conversation.

After we have chatted a bit, how we get back to the business at hand can confound us. Here are some phrases that bridge back to the purpose of the call:

- "Before I forget . . ."
- "Changing the subject for a moment . . ."
- "Let me get back to our subject."

I'm sure you've used similar phrases that politely return the conversation to its initial purpose. We can't control how others respond to our calls, comments and questions. But we can be prepared, polite and pleasant and deepen connections by our phone conversations.

Our cell phones are multiuse instruments and soon will be mini-handheld computers. Right now, we can do tasks on them that were unimaginable even ten years ago. They calculate, wake us up, take photos and videos, play games, retrieve e-mail, as well as the latest weather, stock and sports reports. The application I'm waiting for with great anticipation is the "Phone Chef," whereby my meals are cooked and served, and then the phone cleans the kitchen. It sounds good to me.

While the phones of today can do more tricks than a magician, their original application—the conversation—should be mastered and enjoyed.

ROANE'S REMINDERS

*   The telephone is a two-way interactive communication tool that assists us in staying connected to our network, solving problems and increasing our resources.
*   We must mind our phone manners when we place a call, leave a message, receive a call, and return it, as well as when we use e-mail and voice mail.
*   Clarity of tone, message and information, as well as brevity, are important.
*   Respect the rights of others when you bring your cell phone to a play, restaurant, ballet, party or memorial service.
*   Be prepared. Make sure there's a smile on your face that is reflected in your voice.
*   Be sure your phone tone, voice and inflections reflect your words. "I liked your ideas for our fund-raiser" must sound enthusiastic, not deadpan.
*   Don't let your need to be constantly available and in touch show you're out of touch with etiquette and lacking in common courtesy.

Chapter Eight

Delving into Diversity: Increasing Inclusion

eading a column by nationally syndicated columnist Eugene Robinson made me aware that diversity plays a big role in the popularity of three television series: (1) American Idol, (2) Dancing with the Stars and (3) So You Think You Can Dance. Their Nielson ratings and audience appeal are about more than just singing and dancing. The contestants on American Idol and So You Think You Can Dance, although mostly young, come from all walks of life, different geographic regions, races, religions and ethnic origins. Robinson pointed out that because the contestants are diverse, the show attracts varying segments of our population who can relate to them and see someone similar to themselves on television. That powerful connection is also great marketing.

Contestants on Dancing with the Stars, recognized from some part of our entertainment or sports world, reflect diversity of age, culture, race, country of origin, and even physical ability. Because of this, the dancers draw viewers from multiple market segments. These hit shows represent our country's diverse population just as many workplaces reflect the diverse population of our communities.

We interact with a multifaceted population on a daily basis. While the conversation consists of our words, tone, pacing and inflection, communication is broader and includes our facial expressions, our body language and our attitude. Although we aren't singing or dancing, how we converse and communicate with the people who are different from us, and from each other, speaks volumes. When we're face to face (F2F) in both the workplaces and the social spaces of our lives, we need to make sure the messages we send, verbally and nonverbally, reflect positively.

TAKE THE INITIATIVE

In the early '90s, I first suggested we develop diverse networks in The Secrets of Savvy Networking and further addressed the issues of conversing in a diverse world in What Do I Say Next? The crescendo of communication continues to swell. Diversity initiatives are part and parcel of the missions of most Fortune 500 companies. We live in a global economy that requires not only diversity awareness but also the principles and practices of inclusion. Although it may originally have been the right thing to do, it's now the bright thing to do in order to capture the ever-changing marketplace, much like the producers of American Idol, Dancing with the Stars, and So You Think You Can Dance have done.

Through diversity initiatives and programs, the Fortune 500 firms recruit, retrain and retain their workforce by offering programs that create interpersonal connections and foster communication among varying cultural, racial, gender, religious, economic and generational networks. It makes sense to embrace these corporate goals and commitments in order to succeed in the global workplace.

Robert Cohen, a Gen Y/Millennial, is an audio technician for Las Vegas's Bellagio Hotel (housing the world's tallest chocolate fountain), a favorite of mine. He explained: "The MGM/Mirage Corporation has an amazing diversity training program for our managers. Our team of twenty is the top audiovisual team in Vegas. We turn around setups for events in record time. We work well together, and meet and exceed each client's needs and expectations. But I've noticed that geographic differences play a bigger role than race or religion among our team. Although the two guys from the South are different races and religions, they spend more time talking and hanging out with each other than with team members of similar races or religions from other parts of the country. And, that's a good thing."

Professor of linguistics and author, Dr. Deborah Tannen, found that geographic differences play a considerable part in our communication and are important, as they contribute to common bonds. As soon as I hear someone is from Chicago, I immediately find common interests, whether it's a favorite pizza place (mine is Gino's East on Rush Street), hotdog stand, baseball team (yes, we get the Cubs/Sox rivalry going) or blizzard story. Sometimes it's a reminiscence of State and Madison's stately Marshall Fields flagship store. The person's race, religion, or ethnic origin doesn't matter . . . we share Chicago.

A SERENDIPITOUS SITUATION

Lon-Leighton Barrett, a Gen Y guy, not only joined Cisco's Black Employee Network but became an active member: "The truth is I was drafted. My MO [modus operandi] was to do my work and to work hard with my team. When I started attending local chapter meetings where I met new people, I made different connections and had a good time. For me this was a great way to network with others on my campus and to learn more about the technologies that surrounded me. We've since joint-ventured with other affinity groups. The good news is we get out of our silos and beyond our cubicles and teams, and increase the company conversation and knowledge. Without this invitation, I'd still be unknowingly trapped in my little silo with my head down."

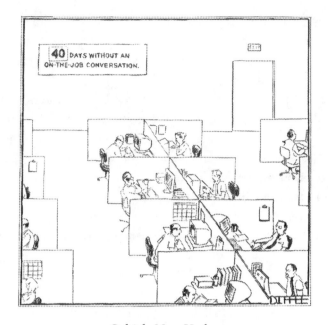

Cubicle New Yorker

As an aside, I met Lon through a serendipitous small-world series of connections that fall in the "you never know" realm. He wanted to buy copies of How to Work a Room A Room for the first fifty attendees who arrived at his luncheon event, and he mentioned to his colleague Mike Phelan that he needed the books in two days. Coincidentally, Mike knew my name because his wife Linda is a partner in Open Book Publicity, and she has worked in public relations promoting How to Work A Room. So, Linda called me, explained the situation, and voilà! Fifty books were delivered to Lon forty-one hours later. Lon and I laughed about the small-world aspects of that trajectory. He never expected to get a call from the author just because he made a comment to his colleague Mike. You never know!

THE INCLUSIVE "HOST"

When I was asked to speak to employees in the municipal electricity district, Susan Oto mentioned the difficulty, importance and need for bridging many gaps. She pointed out that my prior books, blog and programs always focused on inclusion: "You suggest that people 'act like a host' wherever they are. That is a significant way to include others."

Hot Tip

Helping people of diverse backgrounds feel welcome, comfortable and part of the conversation, meeting or project is the essence of inclusivity and is what the good host does.

DON'T MISS CONGENIALITY

Companies are now carefully looking at congeniality, likeability and how well we get along with other employees. Henry Ford was known to have said that he could teach an employee job skills, but it wasn't possible to teach enthusiasm. In an Associated Press article by Ellen Simon on getting good jobs (San Francisco Chronicle, November 6, 2007), Kris Thompson, vice president of Lindblad, an adventure cruise company, updated Henry Ford's sentiment: "You can teach people a technical skill, but you can't teach them to be a kindhearted, generous-minded person with an open spirit." People of open spirit embrace all people, whether it's face to face, on the job or in personal life.

In addition, companies want employees who have the trait that was featured on elementary school report cards: "works and plays well with others." As a teacher, that was one aspect of my golden rule. I gave red checks to those who didn't play nicely with all their classmates. Getting along harmoniously, face to face, in the diverse workplace or play group, is a must.

Recognizing and honoring our differences is important; and recognizing and honoring our similarities is also important, as it creates common bonds that contribute to connection and collaboration. In the face-to-face space, the process starts small. It happens when words are exchanged at the water cooler, in the elevator, in the company lunchroom or at the gym and continues through brainstorming sessions and team and division meetings. Our conversations, our actions and our behaviors are part of that process.

Though it's very important to know and understand group differences, we cannot make assumptions about an individual's attitudes, values, interests or abilities based on his or her defined group. In their book, When Generations Collide, authors Stillman and Lancaster caution us to "watch the amount of [generational] stereotyping" (HarperCollins, New York, 2002, p. 116). Indeed, we must expand their caution to stereotyping of any group.

It's not only good manners but also makes good business and career sense to develop our skills of inclusion and positive attitude so that we can communicate and work well with coworkers, colleagues, clients, managers, vendors, employees, and bosses who are different from us. If we don't have those skills, we may lose contracts, sales, staff support, promotions, jobs, referrals or rich relationships. In spite of the spate of television talk shows that feature pundits who are young or "old yellers," screamers and bullies, most people prefer to work in a congenial, collegial atmosphere. It's like a symphony where all musicians are playing their individual notes while using numerous, diverse instruments to create harmony. Music is the overarching metaphor and model that demonstrates the best traits and products of a diverse team that stays in tune.

THE GENS

Generational issues are the hot button du jour. How we communicate, relate and work across the generations is the subject of books, research and training programs. The emphasis on the four-generation workplace would lead us to believe this is a new phenomenon.

Hate to burst the bubble; it's always been that way. But now we have given new labels to each generation, so it seems new.

Because there are generational differences with regard to preferred modes of communication, most of my clients now ask me to address those issues in my presentations and consulting. That wasn't the case five years ago. The crux of the issue is how to converse, connect and relate among the different generations, while finding common interests, having a common goal and bridging gaps.

Much of our current communication is not face to face, because now we use e-mails, voice mails, text messages and phones. We don't know much about the person on the other end that can be learned at a glance. Technology is leveling the playing and working field. That person at the other end of our communication may be very different from us—and he or she may be a colleague, a potential client, or even the person who signs our paycheck. It makes sense to be nice, receptive, and open.

Age-Related Issues

These days, fifty-year-olds are reporting to thirty-year-olds, and that can be a bitter pill to swallow. It's not an easy situation, but it can work if both parties embrace the richness and variety of experiences and education that their differences bring to the workplace.

Hot Tip

According to Dianne Durkin, president of the Loyalty Factor, if your boss is younger, view that as a learning opportunity, as the young executive has new, useful skills to share. It makes sense to foster a relationship, as he or she will be in the workplace for several decades and can be the person who keeps you employed part-time should you decide to semi-retire. If you manage older employees, assign them to mentor younger employees, and treat them as resources, not relics (Bottom Line Personal, August 15, 2007).

To clarify the terms for generations as determined by age:

- Gen Y/Millennials (1978–1987)—sometimes called "Gen Text"
- Gen X (1963–1977)—sometimes referred to as "Generation Me"
- Boomers (1946–1962)—learned to "Question Authority"
- Traditionalists (1945 and earlier)—believed "Respect Authority"

The term traditionalist, as it was used in Generations At Work (2000), encompassed a generation that has either retired or has reinvented itself in the workplace—that is, people have started new businesses or careers or are working part-time in their prior companies. Traditional retirement is also changing, with some boomers semiretiring. "John Stone" was a juvenile probation officer throughout his entire career and retired at fifty-eight-and-a-half after a final stint as acting chief: "I retired twice. Even though I mountain bike and play golf, doing either or both just wasn't enough." While John has also been a part-time mortgage broker, the change in the real estate world has impacted his industry. Because of his experience with the probation department, he was asked to return and now works four hours a day, which works perfectly for him: "If I want, I play golf or bike up Mt. Tam (Tamalpais) in the afternoon. Sometimes I babysit my grandchildren, and that's the most fun." According to Don't Retire, REWIRE! Second Edition, by Sedlar & Miner, people are staying in the workplace longer in a career of their creation. Since boomers and traditionalists have experience, skills, and connections, it would be unwise to be dismissive of them because of their age.

The workplace will continue to have four generations or more who will have to communicate to get the job done. My grandfather worked three days a week as a ladies' garment worker (tailor) until he was eighty-five years old. I expect to follow in his footsteps, although not as a garment worker. Coworkers in his workplace spanned sixty-five years. He was from the generation who didn't expect to be happy at work; living through the Depression, he was happy to have work. Different ages, different attitudes.

He worked that long because his skill as a tailor was in demand. Zaidi, my grandfather, was happy to be needed and valued, as well as treated kindly and with respect by his bosses and coworkers. He, too, worked in a diverse workplace, with born-and-bred Chicagoans, as well as immigrants of all ages from many countries. I guess my grandfather was an early adopter of working in his later years. Although he didn't talk about his workplace being diverse, he worked in one that was.

"Bring Your Parents to Work" Day

When Bob Beck was vice president of People at Scient, a dot-com consulting firm based in San Francisco, I visited him in his office. He said, "Look around. These young people are ambitious, smart and hardworking. I'm the oldest person in the company and am awed and inspired by their energy. We try to make the workplace work for them. Because most of our employees aren't parents, Scient is not the place for us to have a 'bring your daughter to work day' as we did in my other positions."

Before the term helicopter parents was ever coined, Bob Beck instituted "Bring Your Parents to Work" Day in 1999. He explained: "These young men and women may be on their first or second job out of college. They work long hours and are close to their parents, who we want to feel comfortable about their sons' and daughters' work environment. Because I'm a parent of adult children and have interest in their workplaces, I'm happy to answer questions their parents may have. By the way, many of the older employees also brought their parents, too. In fact, Doug Kalish, our vice president of knowledge management, was in his early fifties when he asked me if he could bring his parents, who were in their early eighties; I said that would be fantastic. He did. We're always children to our parents."

Beck created an environment of trust and support at Scient. He now uses his savvy and experience as dean of business and public policy at the diverse Naval Postgraduate School, which is growing under his wise leadership.

Conversing across generational lines is a feature of managing change and honoring accomplishments. Ray Du Boise, a retired Bank of America vice president, filled me in on the highlights of his interesting career—from being a shy eighteen-year-old only child who entered the Army and found sixty bunk mates in the family, to being a retiree with three different careers behind him. Ray is a great believer in the relationships and the network you must have in order to maintain your position and resources: "I could always pick up a phone and call a colleague or competitor and get the information I need." Whether we now send a poke, make a call or send a text message, we should, like Ray, have that diverse network in place so that we can also get the information and help we need and share the same with those who need our support.

"Aging" Conversations

Generational confusion can creep into our interactions, whether the person to whom we're speaking is older than we are or younger. Part of the Generation X'er versus Boomer versus Gen Y/Millennial tension is a kind of parent–kid squabble transplanted into both the workplace and the popular culture.

After my presentations, young managers and associates often ask me how they can approach and talk to senior people in the industry or firm. Here are some ideas:

- Speak intergenerationally. Learning from those with more experience and those with differing experience is learning without reinventing the wheel.
- Remember that good manners make a great impression when speaking to an older, more experienced person.
- Use the person's title until he or she says otherwise.
- Use the person's given name; do not shorten to a nickname.
- Focus on the event, project or problem in common.
- Ask intelligent, open-ended questions. ("How has your membership in the CPA Society helped you?" "What was your oddest client experience?")

- Offer something about yourself. ("I never imagined that I would get to attend a conference with this many industry superstars.")

These tips apply not only to Gen Y or X'ers speaking to Boomers, but to Boomers speaking to the "Greatest Generation"—and to anyone speaking to an elder.

To be able to meet and connect with clients, managers and professional colleagues of all ages, one Gen Y manager told me that he took up golf right out of college. He found that golf bridges gulfs, and that's a payoff. Sally Minier noticed that colleagues at the Society for Foodservice Management (SFM), who played in their golf tournaments, appeared to have deeper connections. She decided to take golf lessons, joined their tournaments, and in 2007–2008, she was SFM's president. Golf bridged the gender, age and (golf) handicap difference. That's on a par with . . . oops, couldn't resist the pun.

May/December/May

If your client, boss or employee is significantly older or younger, how to interact with him or her can be perplexing. Most people have interests, hobbies, and lives outside the office: they have parents and children, obligations, music and movie preferences, hobbies, alma maters, and geographic loyalties. Find out what these are and talk about them. Share thoughts, ask questions and show interest.

Again, the keys are respect and making people feel comfortable with us. We can respect the experienced colleague who has longtime information about the industry (and may know where bodies are buried). We can also respect the bright, young, energetic person who has a great education and highly developed technical skills. In some ways, connecting in the face-to-face space can be simply reduced to one phrase: Be nice . . . to everyone.

There's no reason to speak arrogantly or rudely in either case or in any way convey an aura of superiority. One person may not be able to get into another person's motherboard, but she may have a top sales record and a few tips to share. The other may ask, "Who is Bing Crosby?" but can devise an ingenious program for the database and niche social network and get the whole office involved in an afternoon. When two people can work together, synergy occurs and magic happens.

In What Do I Say Next? I mentioned that the best communicators are "Conversational Chameleons" who adjust their interactions accordingly. We don't speak to eight-year-olds the same way we speak to eighteen- or eighty-year-olds. We fine-tune and adapt our tones, words, pacing and comments as we should in the face-to-face workspace.

At Cross-(Generational) Purposes

Headlines continue to bombard us like well-lit neon signs of the times: "A New Generation Gap," "Older Workers," "Young Bosses," "Next Gen Conductors" (symphonic, not hardwired hardware), "Retaining Young Workers." Oh, the agony; oh, the ecstasy. The Harvard Business School posted online an article on Millennials as managers. Given their well-documented attributes and flaws, will they be able to take the reins of management? There were hundreds of posted responses, including one from yours truly.

In a netshell: My grandparents thought that my parents' generation would ruin the world. My parents' generation thought that of my generation. Guess what? Each generation manages to manage and the world works! It may work somewhat differently, but it works, because we bring new outlooks, new skills, new awareness and new perspectives to the banquet. That's what I wrote on the Harvard Business School site. The Millennials will manage and will do it well.

In the sociological studies of the Gen Y/Millennials, we learn that this generation has a more open view about people. They're less interested in differences in race, cultural background and ethnicity as differentiating factors. The focus is on shared interests (e.g., video games), skills and vocations. Perhaps it's due to the fact that they grew up with computers and the Internet, where differences aren't visible. The good news is that diversity and inclusion are more natural to their generation. To me, that is to be lauded as a signal of hope for the future as is the candidacy of Barack Obama.

Please, Be Patient

This principle applies to multiple phases of our professional and personal lives. Marika Sakellariou, a former ballerina and choreographer turned fitness expert, is now a realtor. She combines her prior career with her new one as a realtor by continuing to teach ballet classes as well. The music for her classes, which she previously had in her iPod, is now on her iPhone. She explained: "My seventeen-year-old nephew, Dimitri, is the whiz who wired my house. He insisted I get the new iPhone and waited in line for two days for me. He has tried to teach me how to use it. Sometimes Dimitri is not as patient with my learning curve as I'd like him to be. But I'm both awestruck and mesmerized at how much information is at our technologically adept fingertips. We realtors are being given classes on how to sell homes to Gen X and Y, so it's incumbent on me to keep up so I can serve my younger home buyers. It's an exciting time." Marika's attitude is one to emulate.

Hot Tip

Change is constant. We need to stay as apprised and as attuned as Marika, and find change to be exciting rather than a burden.

The "Be Patient" principle goes both ways . . . in fact, all ways. Boomers have to be patient with the talents, preferences, and styles of their parents' generation and that of the Gen X and Y'ers, as well. According to Cam Marston, author of Motivating the "What's in It for Me?" Workforce, Gen Xers and Millennials "view time as currency not to be wasted. Timeframes have to be short enough for them to envision." Like Konstantine Guericke, cofounder of LinkedIn.com and CEO of Jaxtr, Marston believes that Gen Y listens to the people who they feel have something to offer, regardless of age.

Hot Tip

In our face-to-face world, we shouldn't assume anyone is a cookie-cutter prototype of his or her generation. There are analog-adept Millennials just as there are digitally adept Perennials (Boomers and Traditionalists).

GENDER BENDERS

The gender issue is one of preeminent importance in diversity/ inclusion corporate initiatives. Making sure that women aren't "kept in their place" (unless it's the C-suite) is not the premise. The premise is the promotion of excellence, the fulfillment of potential and tapping into the talent pool. All this is done so that the bottom line is bolstered by removing gender barriers.

The era of Business 2.0 goes beyond the basics. Now we have to be smart in how we communicate, behave and relate to the other gender in terms of keeping our client and market share. According to the Wall Street Journal (October 2007), Deloitte Touche (among many other firms) is offering classes to its employees on cross-gender communication with colleagues and clients. The premise is that body language, choice of words and expressions of males are different from those of females. Knowing these differences and how to relate makes good business sense. These programs are having a positive impact on client retention and the bottom line.

For three years running, I was a featured speaker for a program sponsored by an upscale automobile company. They discovered that 49 percent of cars were purchased by women, but 85 percent of car purchases were influenced by women.

This company invested in programs that they shared with their dealers to attract female buyers. It worked. Sales increased' to women . . . and to couples.

In GenderTalk Works, Connie Glaser, the leading expert on gender diversity, writes, "Women hold half the management positions and their numbers at the executive level are rising. Because men and women lead and communicate in different ways, gender tension is inevitable. And, it can be expensive." She suggests that men invest time in building rapport with female coworkers and clients. And women need to cut to the chase and sound decisive. These are two good points to remember as we converse crossgender in the face-to-face space.

Being aware of these differences and practicing these interpersonal skills increase our communication effectiveness. In my e-book, Networking Beyond the Buzzword, in the chapter entitled "From Two Different Planets, Men and Women Communicating," I wrote that, when we're aware of our differences, we can then be conscious of how and why we're connecting with others and what we're essentially communicating. Then we can self-correct and give clear messages, thereby improving our interactions, while being inclusive of the diversity in our workplace and communities.

GENDER/GENERATIONAL GAPS

As I said earlier, in the face-to-face world we not only have a variety of diversity issues and groups, but also each of these social, cultural and ethnic groups copes with subinterests. The overarching difference is generational. Women of different ages in the workplace face generational issues, which may lead to misunderstanding, ill will and reluctance to mentor. I have heard many comments about differences in work ethics, behaviors and lack of respect in the workplace.

Heather, a physical therapist and Gen X'er, mentioned that her employer recently hired several new physical therapists for the first time in years: "What a difference in behaviors. They [both female and male] don't show the same respect for the more experienced members of the team that we did. If they do ask for advice about a patient, most often they negate it. Then, when the department head and I read the charts, we find they're weak on the appropriate progression of certain patient populations. I expected the females to be like I was: focused, hardworking and respectful, but they aren't. The only one therapist who has a work ethic of substance is the one with Midwest upbringing." As a former Midwesterner, I was happy to have the Midwest work ethic reconfirmed as one of the geographic differences I embrace.

We have generational issues in the workplace. But those issues can be a common bond, as it was for my brother. As my mother approached her late eighties and her health began to fail, my brother believed he was part of a larger community. Regardless of economic status, race, religion or ethnicity, the children of aging, failing parents have a common bond and a common cause that unites them as a group, albeit a diverse one.

BOTH/AND NOT EITHER/OR

While some people advocate focusing on our commonalities and others espouse celebrating our differences, I propose we do both. We may or may not meld in the melting pot, but we can create a striking mosaic. While we do have common bonds, interests and issues, we still retain our individual identities as Irish, Native American (Sioux, Miwok, Mohegan, Shoshoni, Seminole), Argentinean, Sicilian, Jewish (reform, conservative, or orthodox), Japanese, Okinawan, Armenian, Indian, Taiwanese, Buddhist, Methodist, Hispanic, Baptist, African-American, Catholic, or interesting mixtures of the above. You get my drift. We bring both our similarities and our differences to the workplace and to our face-to-face world.

Our personal lives are also enriched by our encounters, experiences and friendships with people from all walks of life. As an example, I get that sense as I watch Pastor Joel Osteen's sermons from Lakewood Church. His congregation is diverse in myriad ways, but with a common belief. It's visual and palpable proof of the spirit of his message of empowering our fellow man or woman.

CONVERSATION-ALISTS

For my survey on great conversationalists, I chose respondents who crossed ethnic, racial, cultural and geographic boundaries and represented a wide range of ages, professions and careers. Some were city folk, others farm folk. Very different, very diverse.

What I learned from the survey participants is that, regardless of our diverse backgrounds and affiliations, we're all people first, individuals whose behavior cannot be predicted simply because we belong to an identifiable group. We bring our unique humanity to the workplace and to the banquet of banter. We bring differing levels of expertise, information, confidence and humor as well. The survey also revealed a striking similarity that surprised me. Across the board, 75 percent of diverse, savvy communicators thought of themselves as shy in face-to-face situations. I never would have guessed it.

DAZED AND CONFUSED

Sharon Gangitano shared the most poignant, succinct and common sense advice, as an African-American woman, for relating both professionally and socially with people of diverse backgrounds: "Talk to people who are different from you as you would talk to those who are like you." How exquisite in its simplicity. She also suggests that we make a conscious effort to keep from pigeon-holing or stereotyping people.

To further develop your communication skills for a diverse world, review Chapters One and Four. You'll find strategies, suggestions and food for thought for being a Talk Target and for having face-to-face small-talk conversations that count.

Hot Tip

It's more important than ever not to assume anything and never to talk down to anyone. Patronizing patter is evident in tone and facial expression as well as in words. It's unkind and unwise. We must speak politely to people on all rungs of the ladder. You never know!

A WORD TO THE WISE

How we cope, communicate, and behave with those who are different from us is a measure of our skill, values, and adaptability, which is important in both the face-to-face space and cyberspace. I'll never forget a luncheon speech I gave for a national convention. Afterward, Patricia came over to chat. She was charming, smart and funny and held a very good position in consumer affairs in the travel industry. She was, incidentally, in a wheelchair. She suggested that I address the issue of how to interact with those who are physically different: "As long as we're sitting at the luncheon table, everything is fine and I'm one of the gang. But as soon as lunch is over and I move my wheelchair, people get tongue-tied. I've been in this chair twenty-five years and am quite comfortable. I'm also a good conversationalist! Tell them that they can still have a great business or social chat with me—no matter what kind of chair I use." Patricia said it well herself. We just need to listen.

Food for Thought-ful Communication

Don't avert your eyes and ignore those whose differences may cause discomfort. Initiate. Offer a smile or "Hello" whether in the elevator, employee cafeteria or at the cappuccino cart.

THE (ARETHA) FRANKLIN SOLUTION: R-E-S-P-E-C-T

Aretha is right. Respect is the bottom line when relating face to face with people who are different from us as well as those who are similar. If we don't convey respect, whatever words we use are subverted by our tone, intent, and body language, and affect our effectiveness in the workplace and our reputation in the social space.

We all want to be treated with dignity. The person who we choose to avoid because of our differences could be the potential client who could sign a big contract or the senior executive who hires, promotes, or refers us to a job or corporate board position. You never know!

We need to make sure we give respect where it's due, and to ground ourselves in the basics of civility and common sense. The person who best exemplifies the value of respect is Gwen Chan, who started her teaching career as a junior high teacher in the San Francisco Unified School District. A product of San Francisco public schools, Gwen rose through the ranks and finally became the interim superintendent of schools, responsible for the education of fifty-seven thousand San Francisco students, six thousand employees and a budget of over a half billion dollars. After many turbulent years of prior superintendents' administrations, her interim stewardship brought together political factions, as well as multigenerational, multiethnic and multicultural employees.

When asked how she managed to accomplish this, Gwen Chan attributed her success to one word: respect. Gwen attended meetings even when she knew the attendees were opposed to a district policy or program. She broke precedent and showed up for events that her predecessors didn't attend, because she believed it showed respect to students, teachers, parents and the community to be present. Gwen Chan believed in her product (education) and valued the end users (the children and youth in the San Francisco public schools).

As interim superintendent, Gwen hired her former supervisor

and mentor, who was the assistant to the former superintendent when Gwen was a high school principal, to be her special assistant. She did so because he was respectful and supportive of her during their association two decades earlier. Also, she demonstrated her ability to work well with a divided Board of Education. She politely asked them at public board meetings, which were aired on radio and television, to show respect to her staff when questioning them over controversial issues. They cooperated and her staff was appreciative.

What Gwen did was listen, paying attention to the words and underlying messages of all of her constituents. And that, according to psychologist Robert Sternberg, known for his work on leadership and intelligence, is "part of the wisdom of leaders" (Marin Independent Journal, October 11, 2007).

Hot Tip

We, too, can listen with respect and without judgement in the diverse face-to-face space.

A funny thing happened. Because Gwen Chan treated all of her constituents and employees with respect, it was returned. People still disagreed; they had agendas and issues. But behavior changed, tensions were reduced and people were nicer, even though they were on opposing sides. When what we do is a reflection of what we value, walking that talk speaks louder than our words.

Not everyone looks, talks, believes or thinks as we do, but they all have equally important skills and talents to contribute. That's the good news about having a diverse network of colleagues, coworkers and friends whom we include in our professional and personal lives. The smorgasbord becomes a sumptuous feast; the solo becomes a celebrated symphony.

HEARING LOSS IN THE FACE-TO-FACE SPACE

Sometimes our words won't be easily heard. It's increasingly possible that our coworkers at all levels of business may have some amount of hearing loss.

There are over eighty-four million hearing-impaired workers in the United States. Although they still face discrimination in the job market, the positive changes have been striking. The advent of faxes, e-mail, and now text and instant messaging, and the FCC's expansion of interstate relay service for text typewriters (TTYs), allows users to communicate through regular telephones with the help of an operator. Technology continues to level their playing field.

Ken Gan, who owns an automobile repair shop in Rochester, New York, wanted to find something on the market that would help him communicate face to face with his deaf customers. Nothing existed. He hired electrical engineers and a patent attorney and invented Interpretype, a device that allows the hearing and the deaf to type messages to each other. It's now used in schools, libraries, and government offices, and in Ken's shop. Ken Gan gives a new meaning to customer service (San Francisco Chronicle, November 12, 2007). He found a need and filled it.

Hot Tip

We can make it easier to converse in our space by:

- Listening more intently to the person whose speech pattern is different or accented, especially in the global workplace.
- Positioning ourselves physically to enhance conversation. We may have to create visual distance from someone in a wheelchair so that no one ends up with a pain in the neck.
- Speaking with our face so that our expressions can be read, as well as our words being heard.

Hearing loss is more common than we imagine. We ought to remember that Baby Boomers are turning fifty and sixty, and they have listened to forty years of rock-and-roll; Gen X has put in almost three decades listening to overamplified music. According to AARP, there are ten million people ages forty-five to sixty-four with hearing loss. Research by Charissa Lansing on lip readers at the University of Illinois indicates that some people who are profoundly hearing impaired scan faces for information, looking at all areas of the face, not just lips (Inside Illinois, University of Illinois, October 5, 1995).

Let's take a tip from lip readers and speak with increased animation and expression (talking with our faces) to be better understood by those whose hearing is faltering or impaired.

When Talking with the Hearing Impaired

A Few Do's:
- Enunciate, don't exaggerate.
- Animate words with expressions.
- Position yourself face to face.

A Few Don'ts:
- Don't cover your mouth.
- Don't use your favorite poker face.
- Don't turn your back and talk.

You may wonder why I have written about hearing loss in several places in my book. It's a growing issue. Having taught in an elementary school that housed the program for the hearing-impaired students, I was exposed and became sensitized to the issues. I was fortunate to learn a few simple signs and the ASL (American Sign Language) alphabet. My signs came in handy when I literally bumped into a woman in a New York City deli and noticed she was signing to her friend. When I signed, "I'm sorry," as I said the words, she smiled, both said and signed, "It's okay." No, far better than okay—it was great! Her appreciation and smile made my day.

Michael Phillips, an assistant editor at the Wall Street Journal (June 30, 2007), wrote about finally meeting his colleague and paginator, Khant Lao, after communicating by e-mail for two years. At an informal meeting, he learned she was deaf. When writing notes got to be awkward, he decided to learn to sign—not an easy task. From his article I learned that sign language is the fourth most common language in the United States after English, Spanish and Chinese, and the signing population is also diverse. Being able to sign hello to a colleague opens up many lines of communication. Again, the rejoinder in our diverse population is pay attention. If you see someone cupping his or her ear, please speak slowly, clearly and be patient.

WHEN WORDS DON'T WORK: LANGUAGE BARRIERS LIFTED

There are some people who understand and make themselves understood, regardless of language fluency. My aunt, Milly Cohen, is the best at this. Although she lived in Israel on and off for thirty years, she never became fluent in Hebrew. Yet Aunt Milly never had any trouble communicating face to face with her Israeli and Arab neighbors and friends. Her daughter Sheri, who was fluent in both French and Hebrew, found Milly's ability to converse without language fluency both humorous and irritating.

"In France I'd speak to people in French and they'd look at me as if I were from another planet," Sheri said. "Mom would gesture, laugh, give a universal sign, inject a word or two of French, and the conversation would flow and become animated. To this day, she's still friends with several people we met in France who actually think she speaks French."

When we talk with our faces, we converse with more than our words. Enough said.

DOWN UNDER . . . FEELING LIKE
A SHRIMP ON THE BARBIE

In the global world, even when we're fluent in a language, we must familiarize ourselves with other cultures' traditions and respect their ways. Before I went to Australia for a three-program, three-city speaking tour to present How to Work a Room, I read several books on customs, culture and terminology. But I never could have anticipated my faux pas.

Before the part of my presentation where attendees get up on their feet to meet each other and practice their greetings and interactions, I said, "You can't work a room on your tush!" The responses were snickers, raised eyebrows and some laughter. The term was familiar to the Aussies, but it didn't refer to their derrieres! It referred to a word I would never say in public! Who knew? This warning was not in the guidebooks. But people understand global gaffes, and my audience was forgiving. When my client explained what I had really said, I became red in the face, apologized to the audience and turned it into a "how not to work a room" lesson.

I learned the hard way that we can't ignore the culture and differing customs of others; we must know and respect them. We never want to be "Ugly Americans," even in the United States.

THE DON'TS: WHAT TO AVOID

When we deal with people who are different from us, we need to be sensitive, open, alert and respectful. Following are some phrases that almost never work and should be avoided. A few of them are:

- "Some of my best friends are . . ." (Sharon Gangitano's response: "How interesting. Some of my best friends are, too.")
- "You people ought to . . ." This makes the assumption that we're the experts and have the answers on racial, religious, or ethnic concerns.

- "What do your people want?" Shirley Davalos, media trainer and hypnotherapist, remembers hearing, "What is it that you Chicanos want?" on too many occasions. Shirley is lighthearted and one of the most calm and positive people I know. She would smile, shrug her shoulders, and say, "All of us? Gee, I couldn't say!"
- Don't tell a joke that disparages the group to which a person belongs. It rarely is funny to the member of the disparaged group.

THE DO'S: WHAT TO DISCUSS

I'm often asked by members of my audiences how best to interact and what to say in order to begin the dialogue that is inclusive and interesting. When we avoid the "Don'ts," anything else is a "Do," and fair game. Again, remember to pay attention and speak with respect. Without respect, anything can sound, feel, and be patronizing. Here are some topics that are safe to discuss with almost anyone:

- Your venue or location
- The politician who is having the fund-raiser, the museum where the benefit is held, and so forth
- The work project
- Current events, sports, the organization sponsoring the event
- Weather, books, food/restaurants
- Celebrity dish/movies

The small talk that grows into big talk and relationships is built over time. The real communicators who succeed in our diverse workplace are inclusive, extend themselves to others, show respect, and convey their willingness and desire to make people comfortable with them—no matter what's happening in their lives. Those who endeavor to make people who are different feel comfortable have a gift that's "boundaryless." They are naturally inclusive, not just giving the "illusion of inclusion," and they most often act as the hosts, welcoming others and inviting them into the circle of conversation, the team, the community.

MELTING POT REMINDER

I wish I could provide a magic solution for society's ills. That may not be possible, but I do know that the ability to communicate and put people at ease makes the face-to-face world and workplace a better place.

The "melting pot" is a myth. We're in our "salad days"—a mixture of different ingredients, retaining their individual characteristics to provide sustenance, nutrition and variety to our palates. We all need to be aware and respectful of our differences as well as our commonalties.

If we're smart, we'll pool our experiences, talents and skills with others in the workplace. We don't have to be idols who sing or stars who dance; we have to embrace change, diversity and keep up with the times in order to stay employable, promotable and valued in our diverse global workplace.

ROANE'S REMINDERS

* The workplace is diverse in race, religion, ethnicity, age, culture, language and physical ability—and the keys to communication are common courtesy and civility.
* The secret of conversation with all people is to treat them with respect.
* Talk to people who are different the way you talk to people who are the same. Topics: the weather, the project, the boss, the new marketing plan, the event, the news.
* You never know! The person who is different may be a supervisor, potential employee or client or potential friend.

* Don't ignore or avert your eyes from people who are differently abled.
* Be open to people of all ages. There is much to learn from others.
* Most people are helpful, interesting, kind, and sincere.
* The benefits of being able to converse in a diverse world are incalculable and contribute to our professional and personal success.

Chapter Nine

❦

Group Gusto: New and Old Ways to Gather Together

n an interview for Entrepreneur magazine, I was asked why one-on-one meetings were important for entrepreneurs. My answer was that one-on-one face-to-face meetings, get-togethers and appointments are important for all of us, not only for entrepreneurs. No man or woman is an island; we need and thrive on our relationships with others. Social interaction is good for our careers, our businesses, and our health!

In this age of social networking and "Second Life" sites, list serves and Internet-based meeting places have expanded and enhanced the definition of groups. Online groups and social networking sites are important sources for career and business connections, as well as for our personal interests and lives. The advent and growth of this Web-based world allows us to benefit from information, posts, ideas and shared wisdom. Experiences and knowledge are accessible from a global range of sources and people.

Friendster was the first social networking site, which combined our roster of friends with the wonders of the Web to expand our social circles. LinkedIn has grown to over seventeen million members who connect and reconnect with contacts from their databases and Rolodexes in order to use the Internet to magnify the benefits of networking. There are sites where professionals can glean advice, experience, and solutions from their colleagues in medicine, engineering, accounting . . . you name it. Most online social networking sites also have special-interest groups you can join as well. MindPetals.com and Club E Network are online sites with chapters around the country that facilitate members meeting face to face. Second Life, a virtual society, allows people to have alter egos who do business and socialize within the community. However, combining our online sources with our real-time colleagues and advisors is the best way to stay informed.

According to Arianna Huffington, speaking on a panel at the Aspen Institute about print versus online news, "It's a hybrid world." The same is true for groups. We benefit from those based in cyberspace, as well as those that meet in conference and convention centers, coffee shops, homes, community centers, and restaurants. I have been a member of LinkedIn.com since 2003 and find my circle growing as new and longtime acquaintances link to me. Yet we still need to be part of associations, organizations, and clubs that meet in the face-to-face space. Meetup.com lists many offline meetings and gatherings in a number of cities and it continues to expand.

A Wall Street Journal article (August 14, 2007) highlighted the career importance of membership in formal associations: "It's a good way to land on recruiters' radar and benefit from insider knowledge of job openings." It also allows us to build support and a network, and garner knowledge from what we in the National Speakers Association call OPE:Other People's Experience. Otherwise, we're always reinventing the wheel and sometimes getting our shoelaces caught in the spokes.

Active membership in our professional associations, where we volunteer our time, is one way to develop new skills, expertise and experience. Sally Minier was recently named Vice President of Diversity and Inclusion of Lehman Brothers because of her membership and leadership in the Society for Foodservice Management (SFM). She said, "Because I held leadership positions, was the current president, instituted new programs, increased participation of diverse groups, it was felt I had the right combination of leadership skills and experience. If it hadn't been for my participation in the association, I would not have qualified for the new position."

The good news is that many associations have an online e-component to further connect members and special-interest groups that serve niche networks so that they are both online and offline. To gain visibility, we need to be comfortable, confident and a part of these analog, offline, real-time groups. We need to show up for events, meetings, and trade shows, and become involved.

CYBERSPACE GROUP GATHERS FACE TO FACE

The Web-based world offers us the opportunity for building relationships with people that otherwise would not have happened. At one time, it was the chat room that provided the "gathering place" . . . the living room of sorts. We conversed, shared ideas and had discussions. Now we have blog buddies, post pals, and comment cronies.

When I was speaking in Washington, D.C., I learned from children's author of Letters from Rapunzel, Sara Holmes, about an exciting event. Her friend, Robin Brande, another young adult author, began blogging about children's literature, and others in the field began dropping by and posting. Robin would visit their sites as well: "We would send each other warm, supportive posts and, over time, began to consider each other friends.

"I thought it would be fun to have a dinner party and mentioned what I'd bring to our fantasy potluck. The responses were so immediate and positive that I began to think we should have a real dinner party in Chicago, as it was centrally located. I thought we'd get twenty people who'd come to dinner. We had seventy-five people RSVP who wanted the event to happen sooner rather than later. It evolved into the first National Kidlitosphere Conference, where we were casual and informal and got to meet our online friends face to face."

"It was glorious! People who met each other online through their blogs and postings were overjoyed to have human contact. Attendees walked into the lobby and saw faces they recognized from blogs and instantly fell into conversations. Over the course of the conference, I often overheard attendees say, 'You're just like your blog, the way I imagined you'd be.'

"Some people flew to Chicago just for the day to meet their Kidlit cronies. There was a sense of community because we were around people who, like ourselves, like kids' books. Our conference topics were well received and everyone participated. There's no question that our blogs started our cross-country connections, but our conference solidified our sense of community. We are already planning next year's conference."

Having a real-time gathering of online friends is a classic example of reclaiming the personal touch in the digital world. These blog buddies wanted to meet their new friends face to face. One of the bonuses is that no one walked into a room full of strangers, so conversation flowed. If you have a Web-based blog or chat room group you would like to meet, let them know. You may be pleasantly surprised by the response.

GROUP FORMATS

There are several types of groups and formats that offer likeminded communities of people. When we attend and join these groups, we must bring our best game so that we build our reputation based on our participation. Membership in these groups isn't enough. We need to be visible and have a presence physically, not just online. A Facebook poke will never rival a warm handshake, a face-to-face smile or shared laughter.

1. Formal Network Groups—where the exchange of leads is the primary purpose. These groups also may exchange support, resources, advice and ideas; but leads, contacts, and tips are the top priority. BNI (Business Network International), founded by New York Times bestselling author Dr. Ivan Misner, is one example of a well-run, supportive organization where referrals are part of the process.

2. **Professional Associations**—formally organized groups, but the major purpose is not the networking. It may be educational, informational or regulatory. These groups are available for you to join, if you decide you want to do so. In my careers, I've belonged to the California Teachers Association, Women Entrepreneurs, the Authors Guild, the National Speakers Association and the San Francisco Convention and Visitors Bureau.

   There are as many groups as there are job descriptions. The American Society for Association Executives has a membership of over eleven thousand trade associations. Add to that the national nonprofit associations, as well as regional and local ones, and the list more than doubles. Add further to that affinity and faith-based groups, and the list from which to choose grows exponentially. These organizations provide a host of services and benefits for their members, not the least of which is a network of people who share an interest. There's a preexisting commonality, which is a basis for a common bond with any member.

3. **Avocational Groups**—can be semiformal, and they are the ones you hear about that are not affiliated, have no charter and, perhaps, no dues. They may range from a Friday night poker club, a hiking or biking group, the Lunch 2.0 crowd, a Monday morning bridge and breakfast group to the monthly Six Degrees of Dinner group with colleagues. Some groups are offshoots of online social networking or list serves. Others develop organically. In Marin County, California, there is a group of hiking enthusiasts called the Grateful Dads. They may or may not be "Dead Heads," but they hike with their infants or toddlers in back . . . or front packs. They get to enjoy nature while they nurture.

GROUPS AT A GLANCE

As our careers and lives change, the groups we attend evolve as well. It's important to assess your networks of affiliations. Once you have, you can see the gaps and holes. You can join an existing group, or if there isn't one that suits your needs, you can start one!

The first thing to do is to get a pad of paper or start a new file on your desktop and jot down all the different groups that are in your life. Or you can write on this table I've created for you.

	1. Formal Network Groups	2. Professional Associations	3. Avocational Groups
Professional	BNI (Business Network International)	National Speakers Association (NSA) Authors Guild	Salsa Dancers, Inc.
Personal	American Automobile Association (AAA)	University of Illinois Alumni	KQED (PBS) Multiple Sclerosis Society Mill Valley Film Festival

By the way, writing or jotting down notes is still an efficient form of capturing thoughts and remembering the groceries. A new trend with the digerati, bloggers and authors is the pocket- or purse-size notebook, in addition to a PDA. Personally, I only use and recommend small notebooks that are spiral bound with hard (indestructible) covers to protect the pages. Even in this digital age, we must have pencils, paper, and a pen. PDAs are great, but a notepad can be indispensable for jotting down ideas and thoughts. Jeff Munks shared with me his mentor's advice: "You generally lose that which you don't write down!" So true.

List those areas for which you would like to have a group for brainstorming and exchanging ideas:

1.
2.
3.
4.
5.

Determine if there is a local, national or global organization that matches your needs. You can find out by:

1. Searching for it in:
- Google or your favorite search engine
- Yellow or white pages of the local and special phone directories (Yes, they still exist and will help you locate the right source.)
- Business and special events calendars of local papers, which can also be found online, as well as in the print media
- Chamber of Commerce newsletters, directories, and e-zines
- Libraries: public or company
2. Asking (most people like to help others):
- Friends
- Neighbors
- Classmates
- Colleagues
- Coworkers
- Associates
- Butchers
- Bakers
- Candlestick makers
- Personal trainers

  As I was working on this chapter, the phone rang and I was asked by my friend and intellectual property attorney (yes, as an infringed author, I've had to protect my intellectual property) for a local florist to send his dad a birthday gift. I opened the phone book to florists and scanned the pages for one in his dad's town. It took less than two minutes, and he didn't have to deal with pop-up ads! He asked, got an answer, and I have an example for my book. Remember: The people we know have vast networks of people who we don't know yet to whom they may provide a link.
3. Listening: You may hear or overhear comments about groups, gatherings, and meetings that are of interest.

A START-UP . . . FOR COMPANY

Sage advice doesn't have a time stamp. "If no group exists that you would like to join, start one," advised the late Sally

Livingston, my femtor, in the early '80s, when she saw there wasn't an informal setting where entrepreneurial women could meet, chat and brainstorm. Sally started the Poker Club, a Friday morning breakfast gathering of consultants and others gainfully self-employed. The time and place was set, but there was no formal agenda, nor were there speakers. The participants were the focus. My, what a difference over two decades makes! Now there are numerous sites for entrepreneurial women, and groups like WomenForHire.com and the Downtown Women's Club, which meet both in cyberspace and face to face.

The Discussion Group

Seriously, that is the name of a group started in southern California by an attorney who wanted to have interesting and diverse discussions with people from different professions. Literary agent Pat Teal, my friend and guardian angel, was one of the original members. She explained, "There were twenty-four couples who were bright, interesting, had different perspectives and professions. Our one rule is that members had to be able to disagree without an argument. We have a monthly potluck in the home of the host person or couple who gets to pick the topic for the discussion. Although a couple of people have moved away and one passed away, it's generally the same wonderful group, and we've hardly missed a month in forty-five years." Now, that's a group with a lot of staying power and gusto! You can start your own Discussion Group.

Cerebral Salons for the Smart

The rise of salons, not for hair but for hair-raising conversation, has returned. Based on the famous Algonquin Roundtable, like the Discussion Group, people want to converse, discuss, exchange, expand, and evaluate ideas and information. Book clubs have provided this environment for discussion with a focus on literature. The Commonwealth Club of San Francisco is an example of a formal issues forum that provides its members with thought leaders, dignitaries, and action leaders in all industries. The Churchill Club in the Silicon Valley provides the same forum for its constituents, focusing on the world of technology and innovation . . . which makes sense, given its location.

The good news for those who aren't interested in bonding on the bike path is that cerebral connections and shared ideas are in vogue. Starting a group that meets face to face requires thought, organization, time, and effort. If the informal group or network you start meets a need or interest, there will be ample return on investment. And groups can enhance their offline meetings with online follow-up!

The Coffee Crowd

During the rise of the coffee cafe phenomenon in the '90s, I wrote in The Secrets of Savvy Networking that it had less to do with coffee and more to do with community. Back then, Starbucks had a hundred stores; in 2007 there were over thirteen thousand (Psychology Today, September/October 2007, p. 100). As more and more people work in home offices, the need for human contact and connections has to be met. What better place than at coffeehouses? There you can be surrounded by people and still be able to work and sip lattes in a crowd or alone, if you choose.

Psychology Today recently confirmed my thoughts of the last decade about coffee and community. Starbucks offers something more than coffee. It's somewhere to hang out, and it fills our need for a public gathering spot. Meetings take place in Starbucks across the country and around the world. Dan Maddux, executive director of the American Payroll Association, explained that he held a New York–based committee meeting in a midtown Starbucks: "For the price of special coffees and the snacks each attendee ordered, plus a healthy tip, we held an affordable meeting with customized coffee as an added bonus!"

You could have your first gathering at a local coffee cafe or a similar local gathering spot.

A Network Quilt

Maybe you share an interest in sports, theater, NASCAR racing or quilting. Becky Gordon, a quilter for over three decades, has quilted with local groups of women in San Francisco. They even contributed to the famous Names Project Quilt and My Brothers Keeper sleeping bag project, and have an international group of people who share their craft, interest and talents. It's a fine craft with a history that parallels that of our country. Many of the people who quilt become part of Becky's circle and group of close friends. When in the course of conversation Becky learns that someone quilts, there is an instant connection to quilting of truly common threads. The growth of the crafts industry is one manifestation of our interest in handmade products and being green, where the personal touch has a permanent impact. The quilt world is a global affinity group.

The Lobby Con

The Lobby Con is that part of a conference, meeting or conversation that is informal and has no entry fee. Originally described as the place where a group organically gathers, the Lobby Con meets in the hotel lobby or in the bar for continued conversation with beverages of choice in hand. There are no rules, regulations, membership, formal agendas or meeting planners. Conversation evolves and the group leads the way. In that informal face-to-face space, thoughts are bandied about, information is shared, and ideas germinate. I gave a presentation for a client, called "Networking for the Hall of It," which captured the benefits of what is now the unplanned, unstructured group session known as Lobby Con.

CHOOSE YOUR GROUPS

There are many types of groups:

- Formal leads groups
- Business network groups

- Professional and trade associations
- Company clubs and groups (many larger companies have their own Toastmaster International chapters, book or running clubs)
- Affinity networks
- Civic and community groups
- Informal groups

Here's a partial list for your consideration:

1. For Formal Networking Clubs, check:
- Business Networkers International
- Downtown Women's Club
- Le Tip International
- Locally based groups (check your local paper)

2. For Professional/Trade Associations, check:
- Local Chamber of Commerce and Convention and Visitors Bureau directories
- American Society of Association Executives Directory (No matter what the job description, there's a trade association to join.)
- Google or Ask: just type in a career and group sites will appear—for example, Realtors, Insurance Agents, Teachers, Game Developers, Librarians, Writers, Contractors, Meeting Planners, Graphic Designers, Surgical Nurses, Video Gamers, Search Engine Optimizers, Television/Radio Executives. You get my drift.

3. For Service Clubs, check the yellow pages and their sites:
- Soroptomists
- Rotary
- Lions
- Kiwanis
- Friends of the Library
- Toastmasters
- Shriners
- Political Clubs
- Environmental/Green Clubs
- Baseball or Ballet Boosters

4. For Charity Organizations, check the yellow pages and their sites:
- MS Society
- Leukemia Society
- American Heart Association
- Literacy Volunteers of America
- American Cancer Society
- American Red Cross
- March of Dimes

    By volunteering for nonprofit organizations, you develop new skills, new experiences and new friends. At the same time, you are doing good deeds.

5. For Religious Groups, check the yellow pages and their sites:
- Faith-based
- Church, Synagogue, Temple and Mosque
- Ethnic/Cultural (In San Francisco, as in many cities, we have the Irish Cultural Center, the Jewish Community Center, the Polish American Club, the Italian American Club, as well as those for Indian, African-American, Latino, Samoan and Asian communities.)

6. For Health, Crafts, and Sports Clubs, check the yellow pages and their sites.

There are thousands of organizations, networks and groups, and you get to decide which ones work for you. The groups you choose may assist you in career aspirations; others may enhance your personal life. But whichever you decide to join, remember that creating visibility, developing a network and building a base of business referrals is based on establishing rapport, trust and respect. Once those three ingredients are present, contacts grow into relationships that enhance all facets of our lives.

A Bonus/Benefit with a Ring to It

When a female speaker showed up to our bimonthly National Speakers Association meeting with her rock-climbing gear, I was fascinated. I later asked her what on earth compelled her to join a group of rock climbers. She smiled and pointed to the gold band on her left hand: "A single friend suggested I attend an event of the rock climbers, and I had your same reaction. But she convinced me to go with her, saying that the guys in this group were mostly single and in great shape. She was right! That was three years ago, and I've been married to my rock-climbing husband for over a year." Yes, it pays to attend and join some of those special-interest groups. (Sing me a chorus of "Matchmaker" for including that true rappelling face-to-face story!)

The rewards and benefits for joining groups are numerous. Besides building a circle of like-minded people with similar interests, we get to increase our skills and good health. Research in many universities indicates that being involved and having social interaction is also good for our overall health. Who can argue with a possible health benefit? Not I.

ROANE'S REMINDERS

* There are several types of groups you may join:
    * Formal Lead Exchange Clubs
    * Semiformal Professional and Trade Associations
    * Special-Interest Groups
    * Informal Groups
* Assess what groups you would like to join.
* There are over one hundred thousand associations and groups where people gather to exchange ideas and information, to support charities and causes, to gain updated education and to lobby their cause to the government.
* Volunteering our time for a charity or nonprofit is a kind and wise investment.
* There are private and public-sector, profit and nonprofit, civic, service, charity, religious, and sports organizations.
* Join, attend, participate! It's good for your career and your health.
* We can locate the existing groups through search engines, our networks and the local Chamber of Commerce directory.
* If no group exists, start one.

Chapter Ten

Stand and Deliver: Speeches, Toasts, and Introductions

Whether in our work or personal life, there will be times when we have to make a client presentation, address our colleagues, introduce ourselves in a group, give a toast at a cousin's wedding or a thank-you for recognition we've received. For most of us, it's nerve-racking to have to face an audience and make a presentation of any sort, but it's another aspect of face-to-face communication that we can master. It also makes career sense to be able to speak well publicly.

Public speaking is a way that we can persuade, explain, sell, influence and entertain. The more at ease and proficient we are, the more receptive the audience will be. As it is for many of us, it pains me to listen to the extremely nervous speaker, no matter how well prepared. I end up feeling both empathy and discomfort. To make it easier to face audience members, there are some things we can do to make a good speech and a good impression.

The cardinal rule of any presentation is Know thy audience: whether they're clients, family members, or professional associates. Ask yourself these questions:

1. What is the purpose of my remarks?
2. Why would the audience be interested in what I have to say?
3. Will they get the message and will they get the information?
4. What can I do to make sure my delivery delivers?

As a professional speaker and author, I learned the importance of preparation and the necessity of doing my homework. We must be sure that our information is tailored to the audience we're going to face, reflects the terminology of the industry or times, and is delivered in a manner that can be heard, received, and comprehended.

TOAST OF THE TOWN

Attending several weddings, I realize the importance of the congratulatory toast. Whether it's from the best man, maid of honor, father or mother of the bride or the couple themselves, those words shared with the guests are an important, memorable moment captured for all time. In today's gadget-filled world, many guests take photos or make videos, in addition to the wedding photographer and videographer. We don't want to see our goofs and gaffes on YouTube!

"Here's Looking at You . . ."

Bogie is credited with that famous line, and it's a memorable toast—Casablanca style. However, whether it's business or social, when we propose a badly conceived or poorly delivered toast, it's unfortunately unforgettable.

Toast of Chi Town

One of the best wedding toasts/welcoming remarks I've heard was made by my brother Ira at his daughter Amy's wedding. The day of the event he checked his prewritten, planned remarks with his wife Debbie. When he discovered they were going to say the same things, he rewrote his remarks. Ira made an outline in his head in several sections. In the first, he welcomed his guests, especially the out-of-towners. Then he planned a few lines that were funny; he also allowed for impromptu ones that often magically appear. He was funny, loving and down-to-earth and spoke with the guests; he did not read his remarks to us, nor did he talk at us.

I interviewed Ira for this book so that this terrific toaster could share his insights: "I kept in mind that Amy and David were the focus and wanted to be sure his family and friends from David's hometown in Indiana were included and telling Amy how much she meant to me."

Brother Ira's Hot Toast Tip
"Think about the honorees and what they mean to you, your family and friends and to each other."

When we face an audience to give a toast, we want to be positively memorable. At a friend's wedding party, the guests were asked to share their thoughts. One of the bride's longtime friends did just that. She was so happy for the bride, and it was apparent. Also apparent was her enjoyment of the open bar. She started to talk about the bride who, until now, picked losers, and she continued to elaborate. Yes, it was memorable . . . for its inappropriateness. Many of us squirmed. That was neither the time nor place to bring up the bride's past romances and definitely not her prior selections of not-so-great beaux. The friend is an educated, smart woman who is a doctor. I want to believe that her remarks would have been loving, funny, sweet and appropriate if she had not enjoyed so many trips to the bar!

A good toast has the right balance of humor and honorific. Plan what you will say and use a story or stories that support the purpose of the toast. Practice using the microphone before you get up to face the audience. And, finally, ask people to lift a glass and join you. If you use any of the Eight Great Toast Tips, you will make a positively memorable toast.

Eight Great Toast Tips

1. It's not about us. It's about the honoree. Limit the "I's."
2. A toast is not a roast, so we must be careful about the stories we decide to share and the private information we reveal.
3. Being tipsy during a toast, let alone drunk, could make you as trip up your words, say something you shouldn't say, and put a damper on the occasion. Drink after the toast.
4. Keep the toast to two to three minutes tops, unless you're a practiced, eloquent, and humorous raconteur.
5. Remember the appropriate test. Is this what you'd say in front of Grandma or Grandpa? That test may not work for the bachelor party, but it does if the fathers of the groom and bride are present.
6. Be conscious of foul language. This is a toast, not a scene from one of my favorite movies, The Wedding Crashers.
7. Start with your best story that adds the personal touch of a shared experience.
8. Look at the bride and groom, or honoree, as well as the guests.

AND NOW PRESENTING . . .

If we have been invited to give a presentation, the given is that we're recognized at having expertise and information on the subject. We have to organize our remarks in a fashion so that the people who don't know what we're about to present can follow the logic. The good presenter engages the audience and incorporates answers to questions they might have.

When there's something different or unusual about you, address it up front. A friend who has a European accent learned years ago to tell where he was born so that the audience isn't distracted by his accent. A colleague from Brooklyn makes it very clear he's a born-and-bred Brooklyn boy. Whether our accent is New York or New Guinea, it's best to get that out of the way so that it gets out of the way of our remarks.

Best Presenters Do These Things

The best presenters are easy to work with. They're prepared and will pitch in to help the staff set up and rearrange the chairs to accommodate the audience, if need be. Needless to say, not being a prima donna makes the indelible impression that we're nice and down-to-earth.

People generally don't like being talked at and much prefer being talked with. The goal is to have a conversation with the audience. We can do exactly that by acting as if we're talking with our favorite friend, a mentor or a colleague about the topic. Yes, we do have to have an outline, know our points and know the stories we'll tell to illustrate the points. We engage the audience when we don't speechify. Know your subject well enough so that you can answer questions extemporaneously.

1. Practice your comments out loud, in front of a mirror, and if you want, tape it. Take a walk and talk it out loud. The bad news is you may look nuts . . . but the good news is that no one will bother you. Feeling prepared is the key to confidence. Know that a speech memorized verbatim usually sounds like it. Allow for on-the-spot inspiration.

2. Check the audiovisual equipment and make sure it's in working order. Have a backup plan if it's not. Test the microphone and know how to use the varying types. This takes some practice. The results are worth the time.

3. Send an introduction that is customized for the group. Review it with your introducer before your remarks.

4. To give a good speech that's meaningful to the audience, the best speakers also:

- Have notes (if you use notes) organized before stepping up to the lectern.

- Know their stories and points of wisdom, which they match to the needs of the audience.

- Engage their audiences instantly with a statistic, a fact, or a story that sets the tone for the presentation.

- Remember to add the "verbal comma," the pause that avoids rapid-fire delivery.

- Tell stories that support the points of the presentation.
- Know how to use the technology. When your PowerPoint powers out, be prepared to deliver your presentation without technological aids. At a presentation for Entrepreneurs' Organization in San Francisco during the summer of 2006, bestselling author, blogger and founder of Truemors.com, Guy Kawasaki, found that the room wasn't set up for PowerPoint. He knew his material and his audience of young CEO entrepreneurs, who have to think quickly and adjust to circumstances, so he weaved that into his presentation. His stories were engaging and painted word pictures to which everyone related. Guy Kawasaki is a pro's pro.
- Don't rely on technology's bells and whistles to supplant substance.
- Have a backup plan in case the technology glitches.

Hot Tip

If there's Q&A, include key words of the questions in your answers, because some people in the audience may not have heard the questions.

More Pointers on Presentations That Pop

- Eye contact is essential. Don't look over the heads of the group. The face-to-face space gives us the opportunity to connect by having eye contact with individuals throughout the room as points are being made.
- Reading a speech is reading. It rarely engages the client, the colleague or members of the audience. And you're not making eye contact.
- Facial expression is important (smiling when appropriate, raising of eyebrows, movement of head) and it should match your words.
- Standing in one place can be tedious for the lecturer and the audience.
- Pacing across the stage or floor is tricky. It can distract the audience and detract from the point being made. Moving to the sides of the room while looking at that part of the audience engages them.
- When making a salient point, stand still for that moment.

- Although the lectern is supportive, it can also be a barrier between the speaker and the listeners, and it becomes a crutch. So step in front of it to face the audience.
- Standing in front of a projector or forgetting to turn it off while delivering further explanation detracts and distracts.

Patricia Fripp, founder of www.executivespeechcoach.com, cautions her clients about fillers. "Um and uh aren't words, and they waste precious time and take away from content, questions, and the stories you tell to illustrate your points of wisdom, and can diminish your credibility." I would add, "You know," and it's evil twin, "Like, You Know." One way to test ourselves is to tape a talk, have it transcribed and count these fillers. A brief pause, while we gather the next point of information, content, or story is better and more effective than our audience listening to um and uh fillers. Using notes of our key points acts as a trigger so that we are reminded of what to say next.

We need to be sure our pauses aren't so long that the audience wonders if we have lost our train of thought. After working with a speech coach, a former stage director who preached the use of the pause, I did his recommended long, drawn-out pause in a keynote address. Because the length of my pause made the audience believe I had forgotten my speech, I made them uncomfortable. That was not my purpose, but it certainly was my mistake.

GREAT OPENING ACTS

Being asked to introduce a speaker is another opportunity that can make an impression on an audience and contribute to your career. It's fair and preferable to ask the speaker for an introduction that he or she prefers. Review it with him or her, and stick to the prepared introduction.

The introduction is about the presenter and never about the introducer. It relates the speaker to the audience and positions him or her as the expert and honored presenter. The purpose of an introduction is to set up the audience to want to listen to the speaker. We do that by presenting relevant accomplishments and the relation of the speaker to the topic. The right tone of voice with a smile in your voice and on your face indicates respect for the speaker and foreshadows the benefit of listening to the presentation.

The introduction shouldn't be more than one to two minutes, and it should be practiced so that the words feel comfortable and they shine the light on the speaker. If you feel the prepared introduction is too long, say so. Generally speaking, adding in your comments about the topic or your stories about the speaker can take time and take the focus away from the presenter.

After watching scores of introductions of movies at several film festivals, I would add that practicing with a microphone before the audience arrives is essential. Dare I say, no gum chewing during the introduction? At a recent screening, the film institute representative chewed gum as she spoke. It did not make the best impression and gummed up the movie's introduction.

Because it can be uncomfortable to give a presentation, we need to prepare and practice before we stand and face an audience so that our speeches, toasts, and introductions do deliver and we make the right impression.

The Face-to-Face Intro

Often we're faced with the prospect of doing a self-introduction face to face in a group, whether it's a networking event or social occasion. The same suggestions apply. When we self-introduce to a group, try to add a personal tidbit that relates you to the event at hand. One of the better ones of these "go around the table" self-introductions I've heard was, "I'm 'Joe Jones' and I came here for the sourdough rolls."

When Becky Gordon owned Awards by the Bay, she would introduce herself to her tablemates by saying, "Hi, my name is Becky Gordon. I'm the owner of a trophy and engraving shop.

We'll put your name on anything but you—we don't tattoo!"
Brief, clear and fun. Humor engages.

SERMONS, NOT ON THE MOUNT

Some of the best public speakers give speeches weekly. They're
called sermons, and listening to them is a great way to learn
about speaking. Pastors, priests, rabbis, and ministers study the
craft of speech writing and delivery. There are people who are
famous sermonizers like the Reverend Billy Graham and Pastor Joel Osteen, as well as those who aren't so famous but most
effective. The best among them are also great storytellers. I still
remember a comment from the pulpit made over forty years ago
by Rabbi Benzion Kaganoff about Barmitzuans, which I have
repeated often over several decades. He advocated more mitzvah
(good deeds) and less bar, and the impact of his comment has
increased with time.

The clergy can inspire, motivate, educate, commemorate, and
eulogize. They're wonderful role models when they're good at it.
And better role models when they're not. Why? Because then we
learn what not to do and can avoid boring our audiences.

A LITTLE BIT OF THIS, A LITTLE BIT OF THAT

Variety is the spice of life and of presentations that are valued.
The best advice I received came early in my professional speaking
career from Dawne Bernhardt. After hearing my presentation to
a business group, she advised me to vary my tone, volume, pace
and energy. She said, "You're so high energy." I thought that was
great feedback until she said, "You left me no time to internalize
the information. You exhausted me!" I took her advice to heart
so that I never exhausted another audience.

Another old myth is not to talk with our hands. Talking with
hands in our pockets or at our sides does not add to the talk and
is so low-keyed that it, too, borders on boring. Recent research

indicated that talking with our hands and gesturing creates energy and is dynamic when natural and not orchestrated.

Whether it's an executive briefing, a paper delivered to colleagues, or a presentation to a community organization or to the sales team, being able to face an audience and have dynamic speaking skills speaks volumes and creates a positive reaction. Thus we achieve our career goals. The local Toastmaster chapter is a good place to visit (www.toastmasters.org). A session with a reputable speech or media coach is also a good investment. Check the local daylong programs at your community college for presentation skills programs where you can learn to give a speech or a toast. Then, when you stand, you will really deliver.

A bonus tip for engaging your audiences: Circulate and talk to individuals before you're introduced to present your remarks. It's a great way to connect with the audience members and be your own warm-up act.

ROANE'S REMINDERS

* Plan and practice your remarks.
* Make eye contact.
* Get familiar with the microphone.
* Know the audience.
* Shine the light on the honoree or speaker.
* Start with a story or fact, not with a thank-you, in order to immediately engage the audience.
* Avoid um and uh, as they're fillers that distract.
* Take a presentation skills class, join Toastmasters, or hire a speech coach.
* Thank the host, organization or sponsors at the end of the presentation.
* Modify the intake of liquid encouragement for the celebratory toast until it's completed.

Chapter Eleven

Ethical Endings and
Exceptional Exits in Real Space

While our entrances in life, whether in a new room, a conversation, a new job, or an organization, are important and make a definite impression, in the face-to-face space, how we leave anything—a job, a meeting, a volunteer position, or a partnership—reflects on our character. With either action, we can shine or tarnish a professional or personal reputation; and, the way we exit makes the final impression. It makes sense to bring a positive personal touch to what could be a touchy situation.

PARTING IS SUCH SWEET SORROW

Shakespeare nailed the problem with endings as Romeo bids Juliet good-night by saying, "Parting is such sweet sorrow." In truth, he would've been equally correct if Shakespeare had written that it was also bittersweet.

There are numerous endings we navigate throughout life. School provides a significant number as we move from grade school through high school and finally college. Although each of those endings signals a new beginning, there's always an element of discomfort.

Some endings are rites of passage, like leaving home for summer camp and then leaving summer friends for home, going off to college, moving into your first apartment, or taking a job in a city far from home. Others may be more traumatic. Many of us remember moving during the school year, leaving friends and starting over in a strange place in the middle of a school term. Transitions are tough. Friendships and groups have already been formed, and the new kid on the block has to penetrate a new posse and learn to fit in.

Throughout life there's discomfort at leaving the familiar routine, even if it's just leaving a job we can't stand. The ending isn't easy because it signals we're embarking on a new and unknown path.

The Personal Touch in the "Parting of Ways"

It's difficult to instigate as well as endure an ending. So often we would rather disappear into the night than have the difficult face-to-face encounter. We've read about musician Phil Collins, who sent a fax to inform his wife he wanted out. And we continue to read about e-mail firings and breakups. Thanks to technology, Kid Rock could text message his breakup. But celebrities are not alone in this penchant for impersonal (and immature) exits. There are stories and reports of what can best be described as cowardly, albeit convenient, conversation avoidance.

Then there's the "Post-It Parting" featured in Sex and the City, where Carrie Bradshaw was dumped by a boyfriend via the sticky note. I'd like to hope that was only fiction made up by clever, if not jaded, screenwriters. Something tells me there was some truth to this tacky exit.

I've written this before and it bears repeating: Just because it's easy, doesn't make it right! It shows character to approach the uncomfortable subject. And it truly demonstrates a mature personal touch in this "all too easy to dump by digital" age.

Frumping—a New Exit Term

Another touchy exit occurs when it's time to leave a friendship that just isn't working or even may be working badly. Frumping is the new term some use for "friend dumping." Most of us have been in a situation where the friendship goes awry. Many people avoid the confrontation, which is preferable for a casual friendship. But for a close friendship, "disappearing into the night" does not provide the opportunity to have the closure that we need. According to psychiatrist Dr. Gail Salz (Today Show, October 23, 2007), it's worth trying to fix a long-term friendship. If that doesn't work, a face-to-face conversation, although tough to have, allows for closure and a clean break. "And it's important to be kind. You can say, 'You're a good person, but this just isn't working.'" Elaborating on a laundry list of negatives isn't necessary.

Remember: Ask yourself the defining question, "What's the point?" before you say or do something. If there isn't a good point or reason to do or say it, don't.

Know When to Hold 'Em or Fold 'Em

Determining the right time to leave any place, thing or person requires information. We need to be aware of the environment, people's behavior, organizational changes, industry trends, the clock, and that voice in our gut that gives us so many hints. To reiterate: it's very hard to have to face people when we have to broach our leave-takings. Those who do the difficult display character and do themselves a service, because "closed memories don't haunt us" (Psychology Today, November/December 2007, p. 72).

My mother used to say that a clean cut never gets infected. It was her metaphor for having an ending with closure. There could be a wound that would heal without a scar but never an infection. How we leave is even more critical than how we enter, because it leaves a longer-lasting impression.

Paul Simon may have found "50 Ways to Leave Your Lover," but he might have added this advice for the ethical exit when leaving any situation: "Give people proper notice in the proper manner, and make sure loose ends are tied up." Although this makes a better impression, it doesn't rhyme or make for memorable music lyrics.

Leave No One in the Lurch

Being willing to leave too quickly can make a bad impression on a savvy CEO. Carl LaMell explained to me why he didn't hire the candidate his human resources department thought was perfect for the job: " 'Bob' had all the right qualifications and experience, was well spoken and impressive. When I asked him how soon he could start, he said the upcoming Monday or as soon as we wanted him. That didn't sound right to me.

"So we hired the candidate who said that he couldn't start for a month because he was in the midst of a project that needed to be completed. Bob's willingness to start with us immediately gave me a worrisome message: if he was willing to leave his current employer with almost no notice, he could do that to us someday and potentially leave us in the lurch."

The best job endings ensure that the company or your division isn't left in the lurch. That means all loose ends are tied up, project notes are in order, coworkers and boss know what has been done and what needs to be done. If we leave a job to start a business, it's imperative that we leave ethically. We don't poach clients or coworkers. If there is a noncompete clause, it must be honored or it could cause legal problems. If there are conversations to have or information to share, do so face to face. Never use your office computer to touch base with future clients or you'll leave an e-mail trail of bread crumbs!

How we leave is so important: with proper notice, projects organized, and without burning a bridge.

Circumstances Beyond Our Control

A local nationally known private academy in Ross, California, the Branson School, hired a new headmaster, Dr. Thomas Price, who arrived a year late. Ordinarily showing up late, let alone that late, would be grounds for dehiring. Not in this case. Dr. Price had been serving as headmaster of a private New Orleans school. Shortly after his arrival, Hurricane Katrina devastated the area. According to the Marin Independent Journal (September 2, 2007), "He stayed to help the school recover." Dr. Price lived the lesson he teaches. He had the opportunity to leave his New Orleans school and community but chose otherwise. The Branson School community supported his commitment and delayed exit and entry to their school. Dr. Price knew when and how to leave with grace.

Fired Up

Some people don't want to be the ones to say they're leaving. For whatever reason, they prefer not to make that decision. It's not uncommon to behave badly in order to precipitate an ending in personal as well as business situations. Jane, a retail manager, said that in her previous job with a family business, she intentionally did all kinds of stupid things. "I felt close to the owners and knew I needed to move on but hated the thought of deserting them. It was easier for me if they fired me."

She knew that what she was doing was harmful to both her former employers and to herself. The cost of her intentional errors was steep, and her employers felt used instead of deserted. It would have been so much more classy, appropriate and thoughtful if she had approached the topic and explained her decision.

Shoe on the Other Foot

Empathic people are those who have what Dr. Daniel Goleman called EQ: emotional intelligence. They can easily put themselves in other people's shoes and feel the results. If a global company is laying off a thousand people, an e-mail may be easy and convenient. But, a closed-circuit videoconference, where the CEO addresses employees, who may be in different cities as well as countries, is feasible and more personal. The best leaders do the difficult, even if there's an easier way.

EXITING REMARKS: FACE THE MUSINGS

Here's a better way to exit. Make the decision, do the uncomfortable and use "I" messages:

> ### Exiting Remarks
> - "I've learned a lot, I've enjoyed working with you, and now I'm ready for new challenges."
> - "I want to try my hand at my first love (my music career, being a chef, starting my own gift basket business, working for a large corporation)."
> - "I need a different challenge."
> - "This isn't working for me."

Is this the time for the Sodium Pentothal™ confession? It doesn't take truth serum for us to want to tell it how it really is. "This job sucks." "My coworkers are lazy and aren't team players." "My talents are going to waste." Might as well start singing "Take This Job and Shove It." But don't!

Je Regret

One of my big regrets is that I left my hairstylist after eighteen years and never had the courage to say something, and he deserved better. I didn't need to tell him that he was no longer doing a good enough job. All I had to say was that I needed to find someone closer to home rather than driving forty minutes to downtown San Francisco. But I chickened out and stopped calling for appointments.

Five years later, I decided to leave my aerobics studio of thirteen years to join a new health club. When it came time to renew my membership, I remembered how badly I left my hairstylist and still had pangs of guilt. I decided to do the tough thing and face the owner. I told her that I wouldn't be renewing because I needed more class time options that fit my speaking, travel, and writing schedules. I really wanted to give her the laundry list of all my complaints, but she had never heard any of us when we made suggestions in the past, and she didn't need to hear them from me now. I needed to exit without regrets or guilt. Giving her a viable reason, I later learned, was not only kind but also preferable.

Hot Tip

"You" messages undercut other people, sound like blame, and aren't necessary, no matter how much we want to laundry list our complaints.

Going Out in Style

Some people approach major exits with grace, a very nice personal touch. Newspapers often run stories about people who "leave at the top of their game," whether in business, entertainment, or sports. We read about how Magic Johnson left the court but hasn't left the game, continuing to make remarkable contributions to his team, his charities, and his community. His gracious exit as a player from the NBA signaled a new beginning for him.

Jerry Seinfeld ended his series when the show was on top. He didn't drag on for extra innings in that unpredictable World Series known as the Nielson ratings. Ray Romano followed, as did Will and Grace. The Sopranos left a lot of us wanting more seasons. Pete Sampras and Andre Agassi left tennis with class. We, too, can do the same.

Breaking Up Is Hard to Do

Some of the biggest exits that we have to manage are in our personal lives, and they're often the most difficult. While it's so much easier to e-mail or text a "Dear John or Jean" letter, it shows a lack of courage, character, and courtesy. Unfortunately, the incidence of such cowardice has increased, generating headlines in the Wall Street Journal, the New York Times, and numerous other major papers. The digital breakup is unconscionable!

According to a new survey, 20 percent of young people have dumped someone by text message. In Jane Ganahl's column for the San Francisco Chronicle (May 23, 2004) entitled "Cell Phones Make Dear John Easy," she quoted a survey from Breton Mobile Data Association. It indicated that 35 percent of those who text have sent one to the wrong person. Jane wondered if that meant they accidentally broke up with the wrong person.

Things change, people change, our circumstances and needs change. Sometimes those changes cause us to merely drift apart without confrontation or even conversation. We just go our separate ways because our interests are now different. But the beauty of drifting apart is that in time we can drift back together because no ill words were exchanged. And, over time, whatever may have seemed crucial no longer is. But no matter why we end a relationship, the important thing is to do it in a way that could be printed in the papers, broadcast on the airwaves, or uploaded on You-Tube without either party being embarrassed. Because we may have to coexist with that person again, not burning the bridge is something to consider.

FINAL BLOWS

Allowing endings to occur and adjusting to them, takes an attitude shift, some intestinal fortitude, and the belief that something better is in store. When your final bow wasn't voluntary but was caused by an acquisition, merger or cost-cutting measure, it then becomes the final blow. Those endings, whether they are in the workplace or in personal relationships, are often foreshadowed and are almost never a surprise if we're paying attention.

The same applies to romantic breakups and faltering friendships. There are signs and signals . . . there always are. One of my favorite framed sayings in my office is a calligraphied quote: "What's let go of leaves room for what's to become." When the San Francisco Unified School District laid off twelve hundred teachers due to a budget issue, I was one of them, even though I had tenure. A pink slip from a profession we had been told we could "always fall back on" added insult to injury. But once it arrived—by expensive registered mail, no less—I was finished with teaching. The trust was broken. However, the layoff from the teaching profession left room for what has come in my life and for what will be next. In retrospect, I'm grateful.

Words, Words, Words

Some people need to say final words. In order to have closure, Frasier Crane, Seattle's fictitious talk show host, has the ultimate exit. A booming voice announces, "Frasier has left the building." Some of us want to say more about our reasons for the endings:

- "I'm tired of your selfish behavior."
- "This company treats employees poorly."
- "Your know-it-all attitude is unbearable."
- "Don't call; don't e-mail; we can't be friends."

Think carefully, because those final words can burn a future bridge. You never know! Others find that final words are unnecessary. It's a judgement call. Saying something about the ending may be appropriate in some situations, not in others. We leave meetings, appointments, and board retreats. We end our term as vice president of our professional association. Rotary or alumni associations and other organizations have a "passing of the gavel" ritual that provides closure to help us end one regime and begin another.

Our companies may transfer us to a different division or give us a new territory. Whether we leave a job, a neighborhood, a career, or a relationship, we are constantly leaving behind segments of our professional and personal lives, and, to a degree, ourselves. The endings are part of the cycle of life.

Having an exit strategy helps. When we leave with style and grace, we make a positive impression, demonstrate a positive personal touch and reveal our character.

ROANE'S REMINDERS

* Exits and endings whether it's a job, a career, a relationship, or a move across town or across the country— are a difficult part of life and may be stressful.

* How we manage our exits creates an indelible impression:

- Give a reason. ("I've been offered a new opportunity.")
- Give notice. Two weeks is standard, but give more notice if the job at hand requires it.
- Use "I" messages. ("I'm looking for a new challenge.")
- Avoid bad-mouthing a current boss, company, or friend.
- Avoid burning bridges. Even though you may want to give a laundry list of issues, try not do to so.

Chapter Twelve

Much Ado About Mentors

Having mentors can be a real boost to any career. However, finding the best mentor can be like the quest for the Holy Grail. Wouldn't it be great if you had a person who could help you master the skills, could add the personal touch by introducing you to whatever you need to know and whomever you should meet, and knew the ins, outs, and intricacies that we sometimes call politics? Life in the workplace—and in life in general—is so much easier with that kind of support, encouragement, and education.

"Though I wasn't a completely new kid on the block, my mentor helped me understand the benefits and risks related to working in different areas of my former company because she understood a lot of the dynamics that I didn't," said Kayla Cohen, a Chicago-based organization development consultant for a Fortune 100 company. Kayla returns the support she received and now mentors others in her current company, in other organizations, and in her network of colleagues and coworkers.

According to Michael Korda, author and former editor-in-chief of Simon and Schuster, and one of my favorite founts of wisdom, "Mentoring can be seen as part of man's instinctive survival mechanism. Personal survival can depend on the same process. An older hunter needed a young man's strength for help and protection. Mentoring can be considered an early form of retirement insurance." Or it can ensure you don't have to be retired early.

I know the male metaphor sounds politically incorrect, but it's worth getting past it to get to the meat of Korda's message.

You should build your circle so that it forms a safety net. Some of that building will happen during face-to-face situations, which provide opportunities to meet and connect with those who can mentor and guide us. As a result, you've created life and job insurance. We find these people in the workplace, in our professional associations and in our community. In the school of "Turnabout Is Fair Play," you get to be part of the safety network and "insurance policy" of others. An ancient practice: asking for and receiving a helping hand can be done both online and in the face-to-face space. Mentors give time, share wisdom and experience, and help inform and shape the next (or prior) generation.

I was lucky enough to have Sally Livingston as my femtor as I transitioned from teacher to entrepreneur to speaker and consultant. It's a term she originated in 1984 when I thanked her for mentoring me. "Susan, I can't be your mentor. I'm your femtor!" And, she was the best.

THE BUDDY SYSTEM

The workplace isn't the first situation in which you may have had or given that kind of help. It started when you were a school buddy or camp buddy, either paired with someone older or younger. It was the big buddy's job to help you adjust to the new environment by teaching you "the ropes" (the swings, the dodge ball court, the best swim coach, and so on). While you were the beneficiary of insights (which yard monitors not to rile or which camp sites to avoid), your older buddy would get to demonstrate responsibility and do coaching, caretaking, teaching and encouraging.

While not a formalized process, I'm sure you've helped, encouraged and coaxed others. It may be that you've helped your parents or neighbors hook up their computer or learn how to use e-mail or you've coached a youth soccer team. Or you've helped a colleague with a database program or assisted a friend who was moving or passed on some information and leads to someone who benefited. Now, it's your turn to be mentored and assisted.

If we're lucky, we have mentors early in life. They're the people we meet: our coaches, teachers, parents and counselors. Jeff Munks, the deputy executive learning officer for the U.S. Navy, found his mentor early on: "I was very athletic and played a lot of sports. Many of our coaches were members of the Palo Alto Police Force. During the turbulent '60s, I witnessed these terrific guys, who were father figures, on one side of police barriers and my peers on the other.

"It troubled me so much that I wrote my congressman. I received a letter from him telling me to show up for a meeting with Captain Guy Wathan of the Palo Alto Police Force. And he advised me to wear a suit and tie. I did.

"The meeting was on my sixteenth birthday, and it was life-changing. Captain Wathan told me if I still felt the same way when I was eighteen to come see him and he'd have a job for me. And he did. He was a mentor who helped give me the set of values I've carried with me through several careers."

A mentor is only as good as the protégé who takes the guidance to heart. Five decades later, Jeff Munks continues to credit his mentor for the lessons that he learned. There are several players to credit:

1. Jeff, for being the sixteen-year-old who wrote his congressman to find out what could be done about the confrontation
2. The congressman for arranging the meeting with Captain Wathan
3. Captain Wathan for seeing the potential in a sixteen-year-old concerned citizen

Seeing potential and nurturing it are what the best mentors do. That's also the mission of Big Brothers/Big Sisters, a national organization that matches volunteer mentors with young people who need role models with whom they can share quality time. The exposure to new and different activities by those who nurture the youngsters' interests and their potential is a formalized buddy system that's invaluable.

The buddy system is still in place in many companies and associations. The new employee or member is paired with a seasoned employee or member who is supposed to show the newbie the proverbial ropes and is an as-needs advisor. Their exchanges take place both online and in person, where the connection and chemistry build the relationship.

FRIENDLY FEEDBACK

The important thing to remember is that we all excel in something that can benefit others; age and degrees have nothing to do with it. But we tend to undervalue what comes easily to us. Not sure about your skills and talents? Why don't you listen for compliments? Pay attention to what people say you do well. Ask other people what they think your best skills and traits are. But please don't ask for constructive criticism. Ouch! Personally, constructive and criticism just don't belong in the same sentence. It always sounds like plain old criticism to me.

The best mentors give feedback in such a way that we embrace it with gusto. That is how speech coach, Dawne Bernhardt gives feedback, which inspires her clients to improve. So pick your feedback sources wisely. There has never been a time when someone offered to give me "feedback for my own good" that it ever felt good. If you ever hear, "This hurts me more than it's going to hurt you," run fast!

Hot Tip

Keep a list of the compliments you receive and add to it every time you hear another positive remark. Given that people are changing jobs more often in their careers, this list can be used to bolster a resume. You may hear about strengths that others see of which you were not even aware.

GE BRINGS GOOD THINGS TO LIGHT

Today many companies see the advantage to having formal mentoring programs as a way of nurturing their talented and hardworking employees while fostering the sharing of knowledge and skills. These programs are a good option for formal mentoring. If they're well run and attract people who want to mentor and know how to coach, encourage, guide and nurture potential, the programs serve the employees. If you're interested in having a mentor in your company, let it be known either to your boss or the human resources department. A company mentoring program succeeds if those in it are trained and invested. There also has to be some chemistry between mentor and protégé for the relationship to work.

Everything I've learned about computers has come from several young teachers who have worked for me. They had skills that I needed to learn, so I was their student. In fact, in the mid-'90s, when the first version of my Web site was launched, I paid a high school sophomore $15 to show it to me! And then he taught me how to find it on my own.

In the 1990s, Jack Welch, then CEO of General Electric, realized that his contemporaries and boomer employees were not adept at computer skills. So a reverse mentoring program was instituted. Because the twenty-somethings had the skills that were needed, they were assigned to mentor their older coworkers, managers and bosses—who became protégés.

What GE brought to light was intergenerational mentoring. No longer is it true that knowledge only passes down to the next generation. Much has been written about the four generations in the workplace, their differences in style, preferences, and values. While it's important that we're aware of these differences, we also learn from them. When we're open to mentors of all ages, we benefit. I became a blogger in 2004 because of the advice of Todd Sattersten of 800CEOREAD, a Gen X tech guy in the book business who wanted me to blog about How to Create Your Own

Luck. Nick Urbani, a Gen Y/Millennial whom I met through a Google alert on schmooze, has become my blog guru, fixing, tweaking, and nudging me in new directions. Mary Haring, who has her pulse on Gen X and Y, has opened up my thinking to what's new, different and current. Each of them has mentored my attitude, decisions and skills. So now my blog is advancing and I have a few more MySpace and Facebook friends, thanks to my Gen X/Y/Millennial mentors.

Recent articles have appeared in newspapers about middle-age skateboarders showing up at skateboard parks. Some haven't been on a skateboard in twenty years, but now the pastime of their youth is a legitimate competitive sport with a forty-year-old hero, Tony Hawk, and ESPN coverage. It may even be legitimized for the 2012 Olympics. The "old dudes" are being mentored by twelve-year-olds and learning new tricks and ways of the sport. Who woulda thunk it?

THE PRO'S PROTÉGÉS

Being a protégé is no different whether you're in a new school or new day camp or are a new employee or senior manager or the technically challenged author. No matter where we are in our career and profession, we all share the experience of having been the new kid on the block. And it's normal for it to be nerve-racking.

As I remember it, switching schools in the middle of sixth grade, coupled with a move across the city of Chicago, was over-whelming. A nice girl was assigned to help me learn the ropes and adjust to my new school. To this day, Pam Massarsky and I are still friends.

My first day on the job and, in fact, my entire first year as a teacher at Morse School in Chicago, was daunting. I was twenty-one, this was my first real job, I never wanted to be a teacher, and I had no teacher training (I took the classes the first two years I taught). What made it easier is that a couple of longtime friends, including one of my college roommates, Andrea Groobman, and Mumsy (Joyce Siegel), my friend's mother, were teaching at the school. They helped me adjust and gave me the scoop on which secretary never to approach (and I didn't), who to ask for more supplies, and where I could find the teachers' ladies room. In essence, they mentored me. Starting the new job, going to my first hip-hop class, and attending the first few meetings of the non-profit board I had joined were no different. The feelings of awe, being overwhelmed, and nervousness were the same. Having a mentor can help abate some of those feelings.

Hot Tip
The beauty of the Internet is that we have access to people across the globe and don't have to choose between offline or online; we get to have both!

LOSER AS MENTOR

While it may seem odd, sometimes the person who you can learn from is not a formal or positive mentor but someone who teaches you by his or her not-so-positive behaviors. The interesting thing is that you get to learn from losers and jerks as much as you can learn from the best. Learning how not to be is invaluable in every aspect of life.

The terrible teacher across the hall taught me almost as much as the terrific teacher next door, who made me a better teacher. Knowing what not to do was so helpful. I learned how not to supervise the yard at recess, how not to explain a history project, and how not to communicate with parents about their children's progress or lack thereof. You may have had that nightmare teacher I am describing for fifth grade! The good news is that you survived, which means you can prevail in unsavory circumstances.

As a speaker, I hear disconcerting stories from my clients of what other speakers have said, what they've done and how they treat the audience and the staff. Even secondhand, the lessons from those who are badly behaved are valuable.

The same is true for my authorial world. One of my former book publicity people told me of one well-known author who terrorized the publicity department: "I wish I could say he was passive aggressive, but there was nothing passive about him." The publisher would not exercise the option for the author's next book. That ill-behaved author is a fabulous "reverse mentor." Just doing the opposite of what he did would be appreciated by the people in the publicity department. There are good lessons to be gleaned from bad role models.

BOSS AS FABULOUS MENTOR

Over lunch, "Linn" told me of her great happiness in her new job. Really, she didn't have to tell—it was all over her face. Her smile was ear to ear, and even after a long week, she glowed.

"I love my job and my boss. She lets me do things I was not allowed to do at the other company. She gave me full reign to present one of my books at a sales conference. My boss wants me to meet the media, take producers and editors to lunch and pick up the phone to follow up and even just schmooze!" Linn has already booked a number of her authors on major TV shows and gotten them in magazines and newspapers. She can't wait to get to work each day to learn something new from her very smart, secure and supportive boss. It should happen to everyone! And I'm thrilled for her.

TO BE MENTORED OR NOT TO BE MENTORED

To decide if you want a mentor, you might ask yourself if you're ready to commit time, energy, and the obligation not only to listen but also to follow through. The implicit agreement when you seek guidance, assistance and support is that you will do the necessary follow-through. No one has time to waste on someone who doesn't follow through. If we're given a suggestion or idea that doesn't fit, it's fair to say a version of, "Your idea got me to thinking about the issue. I was able to adapt it by doing ___ (you fill in the blank) and it worked well. Thanks!" But ignoring suggestions, advice and information shared by a mentor will backfire. Don't waste a mentor's time by not valuing his or her input.

If you're seeking a mentor on your own rather than through a company-assigned mentor program, it requires an understanding of what a mentor is: a teacher, a guide, a coach who will show you the ropes and, most importantly, encourage you. He or she is a wingman for the work world and should be able to share insights, ideas, experiences and knowledge. That it should be someone you respect and from whom you will learn is key.

Scanning the Networks

No, this has nothing to do with the techie gadget that magically reproduces letters and photos into your computer or using the remote control to channel surf. This is a "person process" where you assess, evaluate and review who's in your life and in your networks because you know people who are more experienced, wiser, better and more widely connected than you. Some people are so busy looking up the organizational chart for the mentor who is thought to be a guaranteed "free backstage pass" that they overlook likely candidates who would be great mentors.

The "incidental mentor in our midst" is how director/screenwriter Michael Schroeder described the theme of his movie Man in the Chair. Featured at the Mill Valley Film Festival in 2007 and starring the extraordinary Christopher Plummer, the movie focused on relationships with unlikely mentors who surround us and have much to offer. We need to keep our eyes and ears open. It was the only festival movie I attended that received a standing ovation, deservedly so. It was a powerful movie—an eye-opener.

In your workplace, the best candidate could be an immediate boss, the person in the next cubicle who has a certain software program down pat, a colleague in another company or the friend who first told you about the job opening at his company, an acquaintance in your professional association, a friend of a friend who is in your industry, an older alumnus from your alma mater or even a teacher.

I'm still in touch with my high school English teacher, Burl Covan, who opened up words and worlds for me. And he was strict about using attribution, quotation marks and footnotes, which has shaped me as an author who always gives proper credit. I always let him know when something occurs that involved one of his teachings. When you're from Chicago as I am, keeping people "in the loop" is a perfect metaphor. The Chicago Loop is the downtown area known for the late (sniff, sniff) original Marshall Fields, high-rise buildings and the statue of "Mr. Cub," Ernie Banks!

Mentor Checklist

There are several very basic traits that characterize a good mentor. Settle for nothing less. The person you want to have as a mentor should possess the following characteristics:

- The ability to teach
- Knowledge of the organization, industry, or association
- The willingness to share information and resources
- The self-esteem that allows him or her to "let go" when you're ready to move on or up

If you possess these traits, consider giving back by mentoring others.

Mentor Madness

It's great when there's some kind of chemistry with your mentor. But what if that magical mentor chemistry develops with a boss's boss? That could be potentially problematic. One Gen X interviewee, formerly with a Fortune 500 company, spoke of the "sucker punch" she took. Not only did her immediate superior resent that she had been asked to address the board of directors, he also resented her relationship with his immediate boss. She paid for his insecurity and lost her job when her mentor (his boss) was transferred. Her mentor felt he could do nothing to protect her. But sometimes high-up mentors do help you navigate through rough waters and all's well because it ends well. This is what is known as "office politics," and although some organizations have flattened, it's part of most companies, teams and families. It pays to be adept at, attuned to and aware of how to work and play well with others. A good mentor can help teach those skills.

Mentors: Do Not (By)pass Go

You must assess why you want a mentor. Is it to learn, to grow, to be challenged, and to increase your contribution to the organization? Or is it to short-circuit the "dues-paying" process and get that free "backstage pass"?

Too many people view a mentor as the latter. That's not the case. You have to be talented and a very hard worker with a sense of savvy. Unlike an Extreme Mentor Makeover Reality Show or Professor Henry Higgins, most mentors don't have the time to re-create the protégé.

Mentors cannot and should not help you bypass the dues-paying process. They can, however, guide you through it. Much like the trail guide who points out various paths yet chooses the best one, and identifies the stepping stones that are sturdy enough to allow you to cross the stream safely, this mentor guide can't carry you across the stream but may tell you which stepping stones to avoid.

SOCRATIC APPROACH

The best mentors are those who embrace Socrates' attitude about his protégé, Plato: "If my student does not surpass me, then I have failed." The Socratic philosophy was part of a script on a Fox channel's Bones episode, when Booth encounters his FBI mentor on a cold case. "Bones" watched their interactions and shared her observation: "Mentors are threatened when students surpass them." But, the best of mentors know they've been great teachers when their students, like those of Socrates, surpass them. Prior planning and open communication about the mentor–protégé relationship and its transitions are ways to prevent the painful mentor separation trauma.

Mentors are teachers, guides, and coaches who encourage, not bellow and belittle. The consummate mentor was legendary late Coach Bill Walsh of the San Francisco 49ers, who trained several generations of college and professional football players. His impact on the NFL and college ranks is unequaled. His "mentor immortality" is reflected by his protégés' domination of college and professional coaching and a third generation of his protégés' protégés in the ranks. He was a coach in the true Socratic method—allowing and encouraging his protégés to surpass him. When he died, headlines across the country acknowledged his leadership as a coach; and at his memorial, his players, protégés and front office people spoke of his positive impact on their lives.

Donald Trump's firing of his protégé and former "costar" of The Apprentice, Carolyn Kepcher, made headlines. As her celebrity grew and her book became a bestseller, Ms. Kepcher captured some of the limelight that Mr. Trump chose not to share. To avoid such painful partings, find a Coach Bill Walsh–type mentor who savors his protégés' successes.

Here's another bit of ancient history and mythology. While some people think that having a mentor (or several of them) is a shortcut to the executive suite, mentoring has existed since Greek mythology. When Odysseus went off to war, Mentor was the teacher for his son, Telemachus. So a mentor is a guide, a teacher and in some instances, parent-like. At his memorial, several of Coach Walsh's Super Bowl champion players mentioned that he was a "second father."

MENTOR TYPES

Once you've identified why you want a mentor, choose which type is most appropriate. According to renowned career strategist Marilyn Moats Kennedy, there are five types of mentors: (1) peer, (2) informational, (3) competitive, (4) retiree, and (5) godfather/mother.

The peer mentor provides guidance and information as an equal; the motivation is to build alliances. The informational mentor teaches informal aspects of the organization. The competitive mentor is the person with your job in another company who may have informal information about your company and the profession as well. The retiree mentor has a wealth of information to share with little risk; he or she knows "where all the bodies are buried."

The godfather/mother mentor is distinguished from the others by his or her ability to make favorable things happen for you. He or she is a sponsor or guide who can and will open doors for you.

CONNECTION, COMMONALITY, CHEMISTRY

There has to be some connection between the mentor and the protégé. A click if you will. It can be based on knowing the same person or having similar hobbies, interests, and career paths. Although I used to believe that chemistry was instantaneous, time and experience have taught me that instant chemistry can sometimes be merely instantaneous combustion. Real chemistry, where we feel a connection, can occur over time in any relationship.

Cross-gender mentoring was a problem for a male attorney who had mentored a female colleague: "The relationship between a mentor and protégé can be intense and, in this case, the spontaneous combustion was a problem." But more often than not, cross-gender mentoring is healthy when it doesn't cross boundaries.

Marilyn Moats Kennedy suggests that one of the most important traits that the best of mentors and protégés share is a similar sense of humor. This is appropriate chemistry where the only aspect that is uncontrollable is the laughter—which is kosher!

MENTORS ON EVERY STEP OF THE JOURNEY

Having mentors can help us on every rung of the workplace ladder. "The ousted CEOs who have bounced back, like Chrysler's Mr. Nardelli, benefited greatly from their friends and mentors . . . and strong booster networks, as long as the ousting wasn't due to fraud or personal misconduct" (Wall Street Journal, October 31, 2007). And protégés who have ascended the ranks are often in a position to assist their former mentors, much like Gwen Chan did when she hired her former supervisors. Staying in touch, showing up at meetings and conferences or on the golf course, keeps the relationship and connection viable.

HOW TO GET A MENTOR

The first step in having a mentor in the face-to-face space is to observe the people around you.

- Look for those who are treated with respect.
- Look for people who are knowledgeable, talented, and skilled.
- Look for the person with whom you laugh.
- Identify people "in favor."
- Don't overlook the reserved person who has much to teach.
- Look for the person whom you admire, respect and find ethical.
- Look for the person who is open to sharing wisdom and experience.

A protégé can encourage a mentoring relationship. Michael Korda's advice is well taken: "Be a good listener. A surprising number of ambitious young people have never understood . . . the art of being mentored requires that you're loyal, silent, eager to learn and willing to hold back in anticipation of future rewards."

THE ART OF BEING MENTORED

Encouraging a mentoring relationship is an art that requires you to be an apt pupil. In addition, it requires sincerity, work, and the uncommon, revalued trait of common sense. Here are some strategies you can use once you have identified your potential mentor:

- Smile; say, "Good morning" or "Hello" or "Hi." Depending on your environment, "Hey" may work. You may want to rethink, "Hey, Dude," as a greeting. Best advice: know your audience.
- Share observations/small talk (weather, slow elevator, parking/traffic).
- Take notice of a project that he or she has designed or completed. Send an e-mail that indicates your positive assessment, planning or outcome of the project.
- Ask his or her opinion about something you're doing.
- Identify some information or advice you need that your candidate can provide and ask for the help you need.
- Approach your candidate DM (designated mentor) and indicate your admiration of his or her work or work style. It's not "kissing up" to offer an observation or sincere compliment.
- Value the person's time and commitments. Don't consume too much of his or her work time.
- Follow up on advice, leads, or information or you won't get more.
- Report back to your potential mentor and always keep him or her in the loop. Indicate that you're open to future advice.
- Send a personal e-mail, text, instant message or note of thanks with an offer to host (as in "pay for") a lunch. Call to set a date for that lunch or the offer is hollow.
- Encouraging a mentoring relationship takes time because it must be built on trust.
- "Good-mouth" people, suggests Dr. Duffy Spencer. Pass on third-party praise.
- Listen, listen, listen. And eavesdrop, as that is a trait of people who create their own luck.

- Allow the time; be patient and persistent. Continue to indicate that you value your potential mentor.

You can show that you're a good protégé by hard, smart work and enthusiasm.

Hot Tip

The savvy among us stay in touch with former mentors and protégés after the relationship has evolved into collegial status. Why? You never know. The protégé can hire the mentor, the mentor can recommend the former protégé for new career opportunities.

MULTIPLE MENTORS

Times, they are a-changing. Mobility, multicareer changes, mergers and downsizing have wreaked havoc on the "safe haven for thirty years until I get the gold watch" syndrome. You will have a minimum of ten jobs and may already have had several careers. Consequently, the single mentor theory is as full of holes as a piece of Swiss cheese. You need to expand your thinking to meet the ever-changing needs of the workplace. Research indicates that most successful people have had several sponsors, people who have shared their insights, teachings and networks. Those sponsors change as you do. It makes sense that each phase of life requires a different support system.

But that doesn't mean that those people are automatically forgotten once your needs change. Moving from protégé to peer to friend is possible and preferable. It can be done. My speech coach of over two decades, the amazing, smart, classy Dawne Bernhardt, is now a dear friend and has mentored me in my new interest: the world of ballet. And I continue to seek out her feedback on my speeches and presentations. After all, there's always room for improvement.

MOMs (Mentors of the Moment)

I recommend that you nurture Mentors of the Moment—Mini-mentors—for specific endeavors and time slots of your life. Some of these MOMs are part of our professional lives, others are our friends, and some are our relatives or neighbors. I have found that some of the best advice has come from my cadre of unpaid coaches: my inner circle of longtime friends, the Fabulous Four, who love me and aren't afraid to tell me when I am off base or full of it.

I solicit professional and business ideas from colleagues, but it's my friend, Carl LaMell (the chairman of the RoAne Group Board), who reviews and assesses those ideas, problems and business issues. His BS detector is legendary. In his real job, he's the President/CEO of Clearbrook in Chicago, so there's no competition between us. Carl wants me to succeed and he takes pride in my accomplishments. Mumsy (Joyce Siegel) has been a MOM for a long moment—over three decades. And my friend, Lana Teplick, a CPA, is a genius with more common sense and business sense that a room full of fancy schmancy Ph.D.s with MBAs. Patricia Fripp has guided me through the ins and outs of the business of speaking and has always been available whenever I had a concern or question.

My longtime friends and I have supported, encouraged, guided and raised each other both in our professional and personal lives. Your online and real-time friends can also be your mentors. As the old saying goes, "Make new friends, but keep the old; one is silver and the other's gold."

My life as an author, keynote speaker, and coach requires a network of people with a variety of skills and experience: many, many MOMs—because learning is an ongoing process, and passionate protégés know this. If you're inquisitive, committed, hardworking and responsive, and drink in knowledge, people will do their best to give you their best.

Martin Cohen of Calgary, Alberta, is an acclaimed lighting designer for both Canadian and U.S. television stations who specializes in HDTV. He was also a wilderness adventurer long before Survivor was a television series. I wonder how he learned all those skills.

It Takes a Village or Moshav

We need many mentors of the moment, both moms and dads, as Cohen explained: "The summer I turned fifteen, we moved to Israel, and I lived in a community above the Galilee where the men were my teachers. One taught me how to fish; another taught me how to plant; another taught me how to hunt. Because Yorum took me with him as he visited each of the surrounding Arab villages, I learned how to communicate and live among others who were different than I. All of these were life's lessons that I luckily learned. Each one of these men was like a father-mentor to me. In our culture, we assume one person knows it all and can teach us. In Indian tribes, they learn from each man the knowledge that is his specialty, and that's how they retain the culture, the skills, and pass their stories down to the next generation. I'm the living proof that it does take a village to teach and mentor and raise the young."

IT'S YOUR TURN

There are lessons to be learned from the arts, education and sports. That an eager student can motivate a mentor to give more is an absolute truth that any teacher will confirm. However, like the best of parents and teachers, a good mentor or femtor knows when to nudge the protégé out of the nest. When that protégé spreads her wings and flies, she must then take the next step in the evolutionary process: become a mentor and pass on the skill, knowledge and encouragement to the next generation.

THE UNINTENTIONAL MENTOR/ROLE MODEL

Sometimes people have an impact and make an indelible impression on us, not knowing a life lesson is being taught. In an interview at the film festival, on his promotional tour for his directorial debut for Gone Baby Gone, Ben Affleck was asked about his influences and mentors. When Ben was a nineteen-year-old actor, director Richard Linklator sent around the tapes of the movie asking for the actors' input: "If it remains only as I see it, it can fail. Please let me know your ideas." That, Affleck said, was something he never forgot. Richard had invited the cast of Gone Baby Gone to share their ideas and suggestions. This stellar cast included Morgan Freeman, Ed Harris, and Ben's brother Casey. He credited Richard Linklator as his unintentional mentor. To his credit, Ben Affleck listened, learned, and remembered.

DIFFERENCES AND DIVERSITY

The mentoring process is tempered by a number of factors that reflect differences in:

1. Communication styles
2. Gender
3. Race/Religion
4. Geographic origin
5. Education
6. Culture
7. Ethnicity

To deny that the differences exist is foolish. Instead, we must respect, enjoy and learn from them while we include the full panorama of people in our workplace as potential mentors and protégés.

THE REMEDY OF RECOGNITION

Your circle should be varied, enriched by people who are different and who have different skills and expertise. If you cross-pollinate your networks, you must be fully committed and willing to deal with the differences demanded by this global workplace so that a high-caliber workforce is mentored and leaders of that workforce are in place.

I personally believe that the mentor–protégé relationship is best when it's organic. There must be a connection that develops over time. Interestingly, one of my interviewees indicated the only protégé who didn't work out was the one who was assigned because of a company initiative. So keep your eyes open and you'll find mentors around you. And, don't forget, colleagues in your professional association are candidates as mentors and protégés as well.

While most of us would prefer Godfather (mother) Mentors who have the power to make things happen, a solid, multifaceted network may produce the same results because it's full of MOMs and dads.

BENEFITS BEFITTING

The benefits for mentors and protégés are numerous, whether it's on- or offline. Knowledge is power, and so is passing it on to another generation or a peer.

Pitfalls and Problems to Avoid

- Hitching your wagon to a star . . . soon to fall
- Cross-gender mentoring and the gossip it provokes
- Jealousy
- Usurping of ideas by a mentor
- Unrealistic expectations
- Investing time/wisdom in an uncommitted protégé

Rather than hitch yourself to a big star, look around your networks for MOMs. When that star leaves or falls out of favor, you may be out of favor, too. You get to choose and to refuse according to what feels appropriate to you.

Being mentored and mentoring are both beneficial and a part of life: it's the passing of the proverbial torch and the shedding of light. Once you've been the recipient of good mentoring, lower the ladder so that you can help others move up.

ROANE'S REMINDERS

* The relationship of mentors and protégés is rooted in Greek mythology.
* Mentors are teachers who help guide our way through the perilous processes of professional life.
* There are five types of mentors: peer, informational, retiree, competitive, and godfather/mother.
* Protégés can find potential mentors in their workplace, professional organizations, and networks.
* The ideal mentor is secure and can let go of the protégé and be proud of his or her success.
* We can find mentors in cyberspace and in the face-to-face space.
* A mentor can be encouraged by a protégé who pays attention and listens.
* Macromentors are few and far between.
* Minimentors or Mentors of the Moment (MOMs) can contribute to our growth and education without uncomfortably tying two people together.
* There are good lessons to be gleaned from bad role models.
* Turnabout is fair play: if you've derived a benefit from having a mentor, then become one.

Chapter Thirteen

The Grapevine Is a Goldmine: Redux

Some things don't change. The pro gossip versus the no gossip issue has gone on for decades. Some people eschew it and others understand that gossip is part of conversation. It's shared information, and that's not inherently bad. It's the vicious, untrue spreading of rumors that's indefensible. I first wrote about gossip and the grapevine for the original San Francisco Examiner "Career Series" and have followed the frenzy and the subsequent iterations of coverage in magazines, newspapers and even on national television.

PRICK UP YOUR EARS

Whenever I hear someone discount the grapevine and/or gossip, my ears prick up. I continue to listen very carefully to their following commentary, as it's red flag for me. You see, most of the people who stridently lambaste the grapevine and gossip are often the very people who contribute to it. Or they're completely out of touch with the reality of their various worlds.

"Gossip teaches us how to behave, keeps us connected to one another and weeds out liars and cheats. Nearly two-thirds of adult conversation is about people who aren't in the room. Without these indirect evaluations of other people's behavior, society would fall apart" (Jennifer Drapkin, Psychology Today, November/December 2005, p. 56). Whether we're talking about a person arrested for a DUI or the colleague who kindly brings a casserole when we're ill, we're sharing these indirect evaluations.

The grapevine of gossip receives a tremendous amount of bad press, much of which is not warranted. In fact, it's a powerful resource for information as well as a career aid. (In my Chicago neighborhood, the news traveled through our Concord Grapevine!) According to Marilyn Moats Kennedy, author of the classic Office Politics: Seizing Power Wielding Clout (Follett Publishing, Chicago, 1980), the grapevine is nothing more than an informal communications network. That's true in our personal life, as well as in our work life.

As I am editing this chapter, I'm listening to music of good old Marvin Gaye, who is serenading me with his version of "I Heard It Through the Grapevine." Yes, I sing along as I write, inspired by one of my favorites. Confession: I'm from the Alice Roosevelt Longworth School (Teddy's daughter): "If you have nothing nice to say, sit by me." Those who never share items, tidbits and news just aren't as interesting or fun as those who do.

GRIPE JUICE MANAGEMENT

Savvy people realize the importance of informal information. Management experts now agree with the research results: the grapevine can provide you with a great deal of useful information, especially rumors and opinions, as well as facts of the goings-on in your professional or personal circles.

Hot Top Tip
Absolutely avoid listening to or passing on vicious, unsubstantiated comments or hypotheses!

People needn't refuse to deal with the grapevine. Nor should they consider gossip to be bad, irrelevant, or beneath them. Nor is it idle chatter for which busy, hardworking people do not have time.

IN THE KNOW

My Concord Grapevine has kept me in touch and informed about my longtime grammar and high school friends. I've learned when to send notes of congratulation, when to pick up the phone to give support or when to send a condolence card. As my friends' children grew up and started out in the workplace, I could share a lead or referral; and my grapevine was there for me when my books were published. And when my parents passed away, the grapevine spread the news, because many of my long-time pals knew them. The calls and cards of condolence were precious to me.

Through our grapevines, the gossip may yield us information of who is moving, who is marrying, and who is making a career change. You may learn who needs a new roommate just at the time your lease is up.

Convertible Conversation

Through "shared news" I learned that Lauren won a Miata for being Macy's one millionth West Coast customer. And that she already had a car and wanted to sell the red five-speed convertible with a black rag top. I'm guessing you figured out that I bought it. If Marsha didn't learn this tidbit from Lauren and share it with me at Jenni's graduation, I wouldn't be the proud owner of a car that barely holds one grocery bag and one friend. Gossip traveled through the grapevine and Lauren sold me a car she didn't want—and I bought the car of my midlife dreams! It all happened through an incidental, face-to-face, small-talk, grapevine-like conversation.

Bonding Over Buzz

At the workplace, not partaking in or being privy to or paying attention to the office and professional grapevine is a flat-out mistake. You could have the opportunity to forge workplace bonds. In a USA Today article by Stephen Milloti (November 15, 2002), he cites research of Rutgers University professor Dr. Herbert Strean: "Basically, [gossip] creates bonding . . . and heightens connectedness between people."

Hot Tip

- Eighty percent of information in the office grapevine is business-related office politics.
- Gossip can be an intentional leak of information that you should know.
- Conveying a superior attitude about the grapevine could eliminate your sources of information.
- Busy people aren't necessarily hardworking. Smart people make time to manage their careers. Cultivating sources of information makes sense. We're then in a position to make informed choices based on data learned from the network.

Broadcast News

Traditionally, the workplace grapevine has served several useful purposes. It circulates information about awards, promotions, families, illnesses and deaths. That, of course, allows individuals or groups to respond accordingly.

We all have stories of hearing through the grapevine of a colleague's impending marriage, the boss's daughter's graduation with honors, the death of a competitor's child, or a client receiving an outstanding volunteer award from the Chamber of Commerce or American Heart Association. We've sent wedding, graduation, sympathy or congratulatory cards or called to convey our message. Is the recipient offended because the information was passed on through the networks? No. On the contrary.

It behooves us to pay attention to gossip in the workplace and in our personal space. When we don't have that shared information, we can appear to be outside of the in-the-know group. Hearing through the grapevine about someone's potential promotion or probable dismissal can inspire us to get our resume updated and jumpstart a job search before pink slips proliferate.

A FACT-CHECKERED PAST

The blogosphere has added a "Wild Wild West" aspect to informal information and the rumor mill. There aren't fact-checkers as there are in the print world. While the contributions on blogs may be interesting and informative, we need to be very careful in spreading the news, whether it's via the internet or verbally in the face-to-face space.

WATER COOLER CONNECTIONS

To reiterate, if we convey a smug attitude about gossip and the grapevine, over time, our sources could dry up. While hanging out at the office water cooler for hours is not recommended, taking the time to cultivate and encourage those sources of information who meet at the water cooler is a smart career management move. It simply isn't enough to just do a good job in an isolated fashion.

Research on the "water cooler effect" yielded some pleasantly surprising and not unexpected results. People who meet face to face at the water cooler expand their conversations into the areas of their projects. The water cooler has a brainstorming component that benefits the company. Another plus is that people who have congenial communication also work better together on teams. The exchange of casual conversation, ideas and information doesn't necessarily include rumors but can contribute to office collegiality. And the water cooler communication effect can be moved to the local coffeehouse, bistro or bowling alley. When that happens, the gossip can bond coworkers and have a positive effect on teamwork and collaborative efforts.

Off Guard

The grapevine may forecast events through leaks to provide "news of the future," which you may need to know! Rumors move exceptionally fast when layoffs, furloughs, or mergers are pending. Sometimes these rumors are planted to soften the blow or to take pressure off the manager who has to implement the cutbacks or firings.

Today's water cooler could be the cappuccino machine or the video game room—anywhere people gather face to face. To be caught off guard is very disconcerting. When people ignore signals and don't decipher their meanings, it could be disastrous to a career. Having the information, however, is tremendously beneficial. We are forewarned so that we can ask the right questions and observe managers, board members and the CEO. We may even foresee a signal to update our résumés, identify our network of contacts and get back into circulation. Actually, an updated résumé should always be on hand . . . and online.

In the years since I first wrote about gossip and the grapevine in the original San Francisco Examiner "Career Series," there has been much more research on the topic. The conclusion: Gossip is good! According to a comprehensive study from SIRC (Social Issues Research Center of Oxford, United Kingdom), "Two-thirds of all human conversation is gossip, because this vocal grooming (equivalent of social grooming that stimulates endorphins, relieves stress and boosts the immune system among primates) is essential for our social, physical and psychological well being." There you go!

Some of SIRC's other interesting findings are that men gossip as much as women, especially on their mobiles (cell phones), although women use more animated tones, detail and feedback. Men are no more likely to discuss important issues than women. The center's research also indicated that only 5 percent of gossip time showed negative evaluations. A higher percentage of gossip time is sharing information, much of which is positive.

> **Hot Tip**
> Sharing evaluative talk should only be done verbally—either face to face or on the phone—never on e-mail. That is far too slippery a slope.

A FRIENDLY WARNING

Many active professional association members can tell when their industry has rough times. Attendance at monthly meetings increases, because people realize the importance of face time with colleagues when the ax is about to fall. The demands of a job may be all-consuming, but the stalwarts who are the backbone of an association or informal organization may be less inclined to share leads and resources if you only show up when you get wind of an impending layoff or an industry downturn.

> **Hot Tip**
> Stay in circulation, even when everything is rosy in the workplace. Should you encounter rough waters or your personal need for a new opportunity, your potential plight will be met with more support, ideas and referrals. Because some employers offer bonuses for recommending a future employee, continue to hang out and be visible among peers, former bosses and friends.

THE SECRET ABOUT SECRETS

According to a Psychology Today article (November/December 2005), there's such a person as a Talented Gossip. Not only do these people gossip, but they know when to keep a secret. Our country's tradition of gossip goes back to Benjamin Franklin, who started a gossip column in 1730 in the Pennsylvania Gazette. I don't remember that from U.S. History 101, but it makes sense to me! Not passing secrets or vicious comments and rumors is the specialty of the socially adept.

YOU, THE TARGET

What if you're the target of the information tidbit that is passed through the workplace grapevine? Determine if it's professional or personal in nature. Try not to lose your temper, but consider:

- Tracing and confronting the source
- Approaching your boss if the grapevine indicated your job was in jeopardy
- Responding with a memo/e-mail
- Ignoring the information

Only you can decide which option is appropriate. If you have a trustworthy colleague or friend who is a good sounding board, share your dilemma.

A former mentor once advised that denying a rumor was a waste of time. Such a response could serve to "validate that rumor with those people who needed to pass on damaging information." Maybe. There's a different theory: Silent approval could also serve to validate rumors and vicious lies. History is full of horrific events that occurred and continue to occur, because those who knew better said nothing, to the detriment of those who suffered. So, if you think there is something that needs to be addressed, do so. In larger companies, human resource departments can be consulted.

"GOOD-MOUTH" PEOPLE

East Coast social psychologist Dr. Duffy Spencer, suggests we pass on the positive comments we either hear or overhear. That's the best type of gossip/grapevine tidbit to share. "Joe, the team's coach, said you had a great serve." "I overheard Connie say that you were brilliant at data analysis." Dr. Spencer said, "This third-party endorsement builds a context for an exchange and creates a bond between you and the person who gets the feedback. It helps solidify a positive relationship for the commentee and commenter. It also contributes to the relationship between you and the person you're quoting. It's an enormously powerful and simple thing to do, especially if it's sincere!"

WE'RE SPREADING THE NEWS

While the Internet gets the good word out quickly and spreads it like a virus, the bad word gets out virulently. And word of mouth exchanged through both face-to-face and over-the-phone grapevines still spreads stories and news. I received a call from a friend in Charlotte who attended an event and witnessed an outrageous outburst from a speaker whom I know. It was the talk of the business community and resulted in negative consequences due to his misbehavior. A shade of schadenfreude perhaps, but I shared this with seven colleagues, including one who had heard the same news from another source. While I'd never put that news in an e-mail, telling it was a way to share standards of professional behavior at business events, as well as the "mind your manners" mantra. Sadly, no one was surprised at this person's outburst of bad behavior.

Hot Tip
We must mind our manners everywhere. Even if no one has a cell phone with a camera or video capability, the news of bad behavior in the face-to-face space can still be spread the old-fashioned way: people talking to other people.

ELEVATING EXPERIENCES

If you don't want to inadvertently start or pass on rumors, information or commentary, be sure not to speak or shout into your cell phone within other people's hearing range. The classic scene from the movie 9 to 5 with women talking in the ladies' room, not realizing their boss was listening, is replayed daily in work-a-day America. My mother always warned us to be careful not to say anything bad about someone in public, because "you never know if the person at the next table is a cousin who won't be happy hearing your comments." Scarily enough, she was right.

Chix King.

© 2007, Anne Gibbons, King Features Syndicate

Elevators are little rooms that travel, albeit up and down, and so can our tidbits and sound bites. Saying nothing on an elevator can be a smart move (San Francisco Chronicle, May 21, 2006). Some doctors could learn from the silent elevator riders. In a University of Pennsylvania study, researchers discovered that in one out of every six elevator rides, doctors had discussions that threatened patient privacy or revealed information that wasn't appropriate. The docs may be grabbing at an opportunity to confer, albeit in the public space, but I don't want my private medical information to be overheard by someone riding to the seventh floor with my doctor!

GRAPE JUICE

The best product of the verbal grapevine, like the ones grown in California's Napa Valley, is the delicious grape juice!

Hot Tip

If you're not already experienced at cultivating your grapevine, here are some tips:

- Determine who has access to relevant, powerful sources of information.
- Trade information when it's required.
- Observe your coworkers and those with whom they interact or socialize.
- Have coffee or a meal with those who are prime grapevine sources: both inside the company and in professional associations and networks.
- Recognize that members of your professional associations may have information about your organization from their sources that you should know.
- Practice keeping secrets.
- Be aware.
- Don't fan the flames of gossip with opinions or potentially harmful speculations.

Research also indicates that gossip reveals personal values and mores. Certainly it's more purposeful than idle. The question remains: in the face-to-face world, can you afford to ignore a vast resource of information that relates to your workplace and your career? I doubt it.

Gossip and the grapevine are here to stay. We aren't going to stop talking about other people, and they're not going to stop talking about us. We should follow the sound advice of Tory Johnson, Good Morning America's workplace contributor and founder of WomenForHire.com: "People should be careful what they say when they're on the clock."

ROANE'S REMINDERS

* The grapevine is an important source of information.
* Rumors, opinions and facts are filtered through the grapevine. Rumors of impending layoffs are often planted to "soften the blow."
* The information helps you make informed choices . . . and respond accordingly.
* Stay tuned to your sources, listen actively, and trade information when appropriate.
* Gossip allows us to share information and values, and contributes to bonding between individuals.
* Avoid adding grist to the rumor mill.
* Avoid malicious gossip, conjecture or vicious lies befitting those "inquiring minds who want to know!"
* If questioned about your sources, you can either say—or sing— the old classic: "I Heard It Through the Grapevine."

Chapter Fourteen

Sticky Situations

I n most aspects of life, we're confronted with various face-to-face situations that confound and confuse us. How we deal with the variety of people who have different interests, opinions, styles of communication and value systems than we do reflects on us. In this chapter, I highlight some of these baffling moments of misery, the cornucopias of confusion, and offer possible solutions.

Peter Palmer, of Palmer Command Productions, refers to these sometimes trying, sticky situations as character-building moments: "I built it into my wedding vows. Rather than saying 'in bad times' (for better or worse), I adjusted it to 'in character-building moments.'" That's a good way to look at these challenging situations and a fine way to begin wedded life.

AGREE TO DISAGREE

Not everyone we work with or play bridge or soccer with is going to hold the same opinions as we do. More likely, many people we meet will be of different opinions and beliefs. It can be uncomfortable if we're in a face-to-face conversation and find we're talking to our polar opposite about war, political candidates, health care or even a favorite actor, team, restaurant or model of car. When it's apparent that no one is changing his or her mind, move the conversation to another more neutral topic. The solution: simply agree to disagree and find another shared topic of interest. "It looks like we have different and strong views and neither of us is going to change, so . . . "How 'bout dem Bears?" Said with humor, that comment pokes fun at fallback talking points, and the segue has been made.

THE ONE-UPPERS AND THE PUT-DOWNERS

One sticky situation made it clear to me that I ought to solicit others' ideas, strategies and opinions. It's how to handle the person who is the put-down artist or the critic who manages to make the barbed comment . . . in front of others.

One effective way I learned to respond to hurtful and/or pointed comments is to simply look at the person and quietly say, "Ouch!" It's a word that unmistakably implies a transgression, and it's an unmistakable "I" message. Too often we let people get away with demeaning comments rather than deal with them immediately face to face. My team—Jeff Munks, Brad Oberwager, and a New York–based editor friend—has different methods of dealing with the One-Uppers and Put-Downers who not only cross our paths but also cross us.

To the One-Upper, Jeff, deputy executive learning officer for the Navy, will respond, "Wow, that's fascinating," and then politely move on. The Put-Downer is told, "Gee, I'm sorry you feel that way," and then Jeff exits. Jeff prefers being in an environment where people are engaged in making others feel good: "Hanging around people who don't share that value is something I won't do."

Brad Oberwager, CEO of Sundia Corporation, and a successful serial entrepreneur, offered a different viewpoint. According to Brad, it's a matter of uneven power/socioeconomic situations: "If I'm in the stronger position and someone says something negative, I call them on it right away, 'That was an unpleasant comment,' or 'Was it your intention to hurt me?' The direct approach is wickedly effective."

What if Brad is not in the stronger position? "I smile, look them in the eyes, and say, 'Fortunately my confidence is high

enough that I don't need to respond to your comment.' The underlying insult is that they have a lack of confidence and that they
need to put me down. When an offensive comment is made in a
situation where we're equals, I'm very direct: 'That sounded like
a nasty comment; maybe I didn't understand what you meant.'
Often I turn my back on the person and walk away." Having a response in mind for these situations prevents us from being caught
off guard and rendered speechless. If we're walking on eggshells
around someone who consistently one ups or puts down, not
being around him or her is a good option.

My New York–based editor friend is a great "Southern gentle-
man" who usually stays out of conflict: "If the offensive comment
is in a work situation, I don't say much in response, and I let my
work speak for itself. If someone makes an offensive remark in
my personal life, I'll usually challenge that person or say something that expresses my shock or that I'm offended."

There is a caveat to our handling of these conversation killers,
a truism left over from my teaching days. The instigator doesn't
get caught, but the retaliator does. Remember those moments?
"But, teacher, Johnny hit me first," spoken after the teacher
catches Billy returning the punch at Johnny. The same dynamics
can apply to the verbal retaliator, especially if people didn't hear
the instigator's comments. We should be sure to assess each situation before we decide how to respond or react.

SILENT APPROVAL

The dilemma: Are we silent or do we address the offending remarks? If we're silent, do we give tacit approval to the offender?
Yes. When we call people on their stuff, we set boundaries. That's
another lesson to be learned from teachers. When you have standards of acceptable behavior—the rules—the students know the
parameters. No question that they test those rules, but they know
which are the bad behaviors and, more importantly, their consequences. During my last year of teaching, I whittled my rules

down to one rule: the Golden Rule. It may have taken a month or so, but my five different classes of students knew how they had to behave and what would happen if they didn't. Frankly, it isn't as easy to rein in adults. We can't send them to the principal's office, although there have been times I wished I could do just that. But kids and adults who push boundaries try to get away with as much as we will let them.

Hot Tip

Don't be caught off guard. Have a prepared response, comment or look in the event someone makes an offensive statement or putdown.

JEST KIDDING

There are people who will cover their tracks by using humor as a shield. "I was just kidding" is their stock-in-trade retort. Bear in mind my mother's sage advice: "Listen to what people say when they're laughing. Much truth is said in jest."

"So, you actually think that's funny," said as a declarative statement, and in a matter-of-fact but not belligerent tone, makes the point. Or the more direct "No, that wasn't funny" is another option. It depends on who makes the comment, where and when it's made. When face-to-face, your response will vary from sticky situation to sticky situation.

THE TEASE

In personal life, we want to handle the teasers differently. There's a point at which teasing or kidding around becomes tormenting or bullying. According to Dr. Hara Estroff Marano (Psychology Today, March/April 2006, p. 51), we need to "determine if the kidding taps a reservoir of nastiness and if the perpetrator teases in other contexts." If so, banter right along, but when the propitious moment presents itself, mention your reaction to the comments and how the remarks make you feel.

1. "I am really uncomfortable."
2. "I find zingers to be . . ."
3. "I would prefer if . . ."
4. "What was that about?"

Dr. Geraldine Alpert, a Marin County, California, psychologist, advises not to smile as we make our statements. The smile sends a mixed message to the person who already has demonstrated a lack of awareness or indifference. Not smiling makes our message crystal clear.

BIG BROTHER (AND SISTER) ARE WATCHING

There are varying ways to respond to sticky situations, but there's one thing to remember: how we comport ourselves in public is easily captured for all times. Now we can be videoed on cell phones and uploaded without our consent. The watchword: If we prefer not to be seen doing whatever on YouTube, we just don't do it! Think about Seinfeld's Kramer's (Michael Richard's) rant and what happened to his career after the controversy. His outburst of racial epithets was caught on a cell phone and uploaded to YouTube. The rest is history, as was his career. Though Richard may resurrect his career, other people have lost jobs, professional careers have collapsed, and relationships have been ruined because their moment of "losing it," in whatever fashion, will never be forgotten.

BRIDGING CONVERSATION AND CULTURES

Sometimes a good deed could go awry, but it doesn't. On vacation in Minnesota after a horrendous bridge catastrophe in the summer of 2007, my friend Kathleen was one of many tourists walking another bridge that had a view of the collapsed bridge. She saw a father taking a photo of his wife and kids and offered to take a photo of the whole family. They were delighted. Kathleen took the perfectly framed photo. As she showed it to them, Kathleen said, "This would make a great Christmas card." Her New York travel companions informed her that she goofed and missed the clues: they could tell by the family's attire that they were an Orthodox Jewish family who didn't celebrate Christmas. Kathleen was mortified.

When I asked Kathleen what the woman said when Kathleen showed her the photo and made the Christmas comment, the answer was perfect: "Thank you so very much." She valued the kindness Kathleen displayed by offering to take the family photo and didn't try to educate Kathleen on the innocent politically incorrect comment. She did what an appreciative, kind, savvy person would do: she said, "Thank you." They were two thoughtful people treating each other with respect. That's an example of what could have been a sticky situation and how it was resolved with grace in the face-to-face space.

TWISTING IN THE WIND

Any one of us who has waited to hear if our job interview landed us a job, if our proposal was accepted by our client, or if our application was accepted by a school knows how stressful, annoying or just plain difficult it is to wait. It's equally difficult for the executive or manager who has offered a candidate a job to wait to hear if he or she accepts the offer. The no-response gambit is unacceptable; saying nothing is an avoidance behavior to avoid. For many of us, living in limbo is rarely our first choice. Most people prefer having closure and would rather know the decision, even if it's not the one they wanted.

> **Hot Tip**
> Whether it's face to face or on the phone, hearing a decision or an outcome is a relief. It's also a courtesy we give to people so that we don't leave others in limbo.

Lois Keenan, a program manager in Solano, California, was hiring staff for the county deaf/hard-of-hearing program: "It's always a challenge to fill our positions before the new school year begins. I thought I had found the perfect candidate. She was from out of state and wanted to move to California. Her credentials were impeccable, and I had a gut-level feeling that there was a connection. I got permission to have her send a video rather than conduct an in-person interview, so we were able to see she was fluent in sign language, which is a prerequisite for these teaching positions.

"The conversations/interviews went well and I had confidence in her. Mind you, we have to have everyone in place well before the school year begins. I called twice to follow up and left enthusiastic messages on her machine. But there was no response. I went out on a limb for her with my boss. I trusted my gut feeling based on our conversations. Finally, the HR department reached her and learned she decided not to move to California at this time. All she had to do was call back. If that was out of her comfort level, at least she could have sent me an e-mail so I could have amped up the search process. That would have been the thoughtful, mature thing to do. Instead, she left me in limbo."

The deaf/hard-of-hearing education community is a tightly knit network. People share information, sources, and recommendations all the time. No matter how uncomfortable the "I must turn you down this time" call is, making that connection reflects character. Lois Keenan adds, "If she couldn't face talking to me directly, she could at least have called after office hours and left a message." She will be one name that won't be forgotten!

LAP-TOPPLED JUDGEMENTS

At some dinner parties, the laptop has become the uninvited guest, according to the New York Observer (July 30, 2007, p. C5) in an article entitled "MAC and Cheese." It would be a mistake to assume the "guess what's coming to dinner" is only a New York quirk, as the laptopic is occurring in other parts of the country, including the San Francisco Bay area. According to journalist, Meredith Bryan, "A certain social ability quotient is lost when the laptop takes over. We no longer have to be interesting, fun, or attentive. YouTube does that for us."

When people plan a guest list of people who will click and they go to the trouble of providing a meal, guests ought to respect the host. Unless you're invited to "bring a guest or your laptop," leave them at home. In this age of instant information, we may feel we need to confirm a statement immediately. It could be okay to check the laptop, if that's a socially acceptable dinner party dynamic in your crowd and with your host. However, texting or e-mailing people who aren't at the dinner party is often perceived as rude. The subtext is "someone not here is more interesting than those of you who are here." Leave the techie tools off the dinner party table.

DIALING IT DOWN

Cubicle life means constant exposure to other people's noise. In some cases, there's less space between them than between two cells in a jail! Whether it's a loud conversation or music, excessive volume can add to volatility. Add a cell phone to the mix and you're in a "loud talker torture chamber."

Cubicle life presents other potentially sticky situations, according to a survey of cubicle affronts by staffing firm Randstad USA: potent scents, such as perfume, "l'air du cigarettes," or pungent, spicy foods; overuse of personal communication devices and misuse of e-mail, especially the "Reply to All" button. Interestingly enough, gossip was mentioned as the top annoyance if someone is in an open pod. But what was dubbed as gossip may be nothing more than a loud newsy exchange of information: a mere conversation. If someone is intensely working on a project, noise can mean a loud exchange about the weather. It isn't gossip, but in close cubicle quarters, it may well be annoying (San Francisco Chronicle, October 31, 2007).

It makes sense to realize that one reason people talk loudly could be attributed to a hearing loss. A colleague has a voice that's so loud and carries so far, it's apparent that the years of rock concerts have taken a toll. But cubicle life amplifies noise. Some people aren't aware and would gladly adjust their volume. It's best to say something kindly, clearly, and, dare I say it again, using "I" messages. That's not the time to point a finger and use the "You" message. Although it may be easier to send an e-mail, don't. Get up, walk over and say something face to face. The e-mail most likely will not be read with the tone you intended.

Hot Tip

Avoid:

- "You're too loud."
- "You're ruining my concentration."
- "You're disturbing the peace."
- "Pipe down."

Use:

- "I'm having trouble concentrating."
- "I would really appreciate it if you'd lower your voice/music."

WHEN WE BLUNDER

There are times that the mistake is ours. Inadvertently, we may misspeak or misstep. Whether we say or do something inappropriate, there's only one course of remedy. Fess up!

1. Take responsibility. "My error. I don't know . . . how that got by me"; "why I said that (or what made me think or do that)." "My bad" is not the right comment, as it makes light of your error.
2. Apologize sincerely. Avoid the half-baked and thoroughly spun verbiage of the infamous public offenders who skirt the issue. Direct and clear is best: "My sincere apology. I am so sorry I said or did _____ (you fill in the blank). It was never my intention to hurt, embarrass, etc., you." Tone, inflection and facial expression all must match. Avoid: "I hope you weren't upset" or "I hope you weren't offended." They're "You" statements that slough off the responsibility onto the offended person. People are more forgiving when the apology is a real one. Just as we accept the sincere apologies of others, so will they accept ours.

QUESTION-ABLE BEHAVIOR

There are those people who claim interest and curiosity as they pry and probe when in person. Gail Toppel, a Los Angeles attorney, learned how to handle this sticky situation from a law school classmate and longtime friend: "If someone asked her a question she didn't want to answer, she changed the subject. If the person persisted, my friend would very calmly and very nicely say, 'I thought you would realize that when I didn't answer, your question was one I consider personal.'" Gail further added that she personally will sometimes ask, "Why would you want to know?" It's also fair to say, "I prefer not to answer personal questions." Although these responses aren't said in an irritated tone, they usually put an end to the prying.

HANDLING THE DIFFICULT QUESTION

Sometimes we're asked questions that are difficult to answer for whatever reason. This happens in the workplace and in our personal lives, and it can catch us off guard. An article by Matthew Hutson in Psychology Today (November/December 2007, p. 15) recommends that in order to retrieve information or formulate a response, you should look away before answering. Studies show it will improve your concentration. Because the brain has a hard time ignoring others' faces, looking away blocks the distraction. But don't look away too long, as that could be considered rude.

THE BRAG DRAG-ON

There are some people who hesitate to say very much about themselves lest it sound like bragging. And then there are others whose every declarative sentence sounds like a boast. Whether it's about the zeroes in their latest bonus, client deal, job offer package, home appraisal, techno stock options or cost of the newest techie gadget or bling, I, for one, am tired of hearing the "brag-on dragon." A conversation with a colleague in which he mentioned for the third time his six-figure deal with a client got on my last nerve. I finally said something, but it was a much-too-subtle innuendo (and I thought it was a wildly funny comment). I was baffled. Do I tell him to stop the bragging, or like my grandmother might have said, "Enough already"? One suggestion came from Miss Manners. In my upbeat voice, I could say, "Well, good for you," and change the subject.

Jane, a director of sales for several different companies, has heard a lot of interesting bragging among her team and her bosses. "One of the comments I will make is 'That's really none of my business,' which I say matter of factly." Jane also will say that when way too much information is being off-loaded by a date. "When a fellow starts to tell me the cause of his divorce and talk about his former wife, I'll say, 'I'm uncomfortable because that's personal and really none of my business.' And the off-loading and bad mouthing stops."

I ran this sticky bragging situation by Sherwood Cummins, founder of Recreate, who is my personal trainer and a Presbyterian minister, whose wisdom and pastoral counseling are insightful. When I asked him what compelled these show-offs to brag in dollar signs, he thoughtfully assessed my question: "People who brag do so to get the world to mirror to them that they're great. So once their greatness is mirrored back to them, they'll believe they really are wonderful. Sadly, they never do."

In this sticky situation, when someone is in our face bragging, we could simply ask, "Why are you telling me this?" That would give the person who is prone to bragging plenty of food for thought.

DEALING WITH THE DEROGATORY

In a perfect world, I wouldn't have to include this issue in this chapter. In our face-to-face world, the derogatory comment, the personal slur, continues to be uttered. It could be the "you people" blatant stereotypical statement as was recently said to Joyce Siegel, an octogenarian who's known for her charm, kindness and affability. She's played bridge at the same club for over thirty years. The fellow who leveled his derogatory statement had known Mrs. Siegel for years and had always been pleasant. She said, "We all knew he had anger management problems and was getting help for it. But when he uttered his 'you people' comment, I just froze. I said absolutely nothing and neither did my partners. It's one thing to understand that a person has anger issues, but quite another to hear a stereotypical, prejudicial slur. About fifteen minutes later, he came over and apologized, explaining he was getting help for his temper. What's there to say? 'Oh, it's all right.' No, nothing was all right, so I said nothing. And I will not initiate any contact or conversation in the future." When I asked Mrs. Siegel what she'll do if he talks to her, she said she would nod, return the hello so as not to cause tension among other club members, but that's all.

Being perfunctorily polite so as not to cause discomfort to others in the group is wise and considerate. It shows grace in the personal face-to-face space. But this is beyond a sticky situation; it's a stinking one. Here are several other possible responses to unseemly situations:

1. Give "the look" and walk away.
2. Make a comment without a smile:
   - "It's unfortunate you feel that way."
   - "I never expected to hear such a comment from you."
   - "I'm taken aback that you would say such a thing."
3. Use the tone of humor, and lightly and clearly say, "I had no idea you were one of those kinds of people!" and walk away.

If You Aren't One of the "You People"

There are times we hear the slur about someone or some group and it bothers us on a number of levels, even though we're not a member of that defamed group. Do we stay silent? Give a tongue lashing? Tell the person off? Only you can answer this question. How will you feel later if you do/don't say something now? This is the most important question to ask yourself. Here are some statements that you could say:

- "That's not the way I see it."
- "That's not been my experience."
- "I don't see how we can make a wholesale statement of condemnation."
- "Those are harsh words."
- "I find the opposite to be true."

This is where we can proudly be old school, because those who have "old school manners, breeding and polish don't tolerate careless talk about good people" (Men's Health Magazine, Rodale Publishing, June 16, 2006).

Tell Tale Tattling

The age-old dilemma rears its ugly head when we see, know or hear something that's not positive. Should we share the message or keep it to ourselves? Many years ago, I saw a friend's husband at a convention with his arms lovingly around another woman. In my naiveté, I had assumed it was his doppelganger and not the man married to my friend. Several months later, in a conversation with a mutual friend, it hit me . . . that was "Ted" and not his stunt double. What to do? What to say?

Decisions, decisions. I chose not to say anything. They were married with three young children, and my friend was happy. What I saw could possibly have had a reasonable explanation, although, to this day, none comes to mind. But, more importantly, would this bit of news accomplish anything? Yes, my friend would know her guy was not the man we thought he was, and a family could be destroyed. Perhaps I was gutless. However, there is other bad news I have shared when it was appropriate to do so: telling of a death of a friend's parent, an illness discovered by a relative, and so on. That kind of news rallies the support of the troops. But this was different.

I sometimes wonder what would have happened had I come from the school of blurting out bad news. It's twenty-three years later and my friend is still married. I can still, in my mind's eye, see him at that event being untrue to my friend. But they're now grandparents who together happily enjoy their children, grand-children, and extended family. It makes me pleased that I had chosen not to deliver the bad news.

Sometimes we have to think about the long-term results of a short-lived moment.

When to Be Wishy-Washy

Believe it or not, there are times when it's better not to chime in, not to mention an opinion, not to add our "two cents worth," as it makes the situation stickier. When a friend is venting about a job, a spouse or significant other, or a coworker, just listen. Sheila was venting about her husband. After listening to Sheila vent, her sister chimed in with more corroborative insights, adding fuel to the flame. Sheila turned to her sister and said, "All I wanted was for you to listen, not to say anything."

If we join in the badmouthing and the couple gets back on track, the person will never forget what we said. Best bet: In this sticky situation, be all ears and no mouth.

HEALTH CARE-ING ABOUT OURSELVES

Being in charge of our own health care often means we have to advocate for ourselves even when we're not feeling well. Dr. Sara Skolnick finds that some of her patients aren't forthcoming in the face-to-face interview/exam: "It's important that patients are comfortable, have notes prepared so that they mention their issues and symptoms and ask their questions. That helps me pro-vide the medical care they need." For a more serious medical situ-ation, having a friend or relative with you as an advocate is a good idea. This person can hear what we might not, ask the questions we forget to ask, and refocus back to the issue at hand.

Dr. Jerome Groopman, author of How Doctors Think (Houghton Mifflin, New York, 2007), suggests that patients tell their whole story, because the doctor may not know which symptom is the root of the problem. A 1984 study showed that doctors interrupt patients after eighteen seconds to make a diagnosis, and these fast responses contribute to the 15 to 20 percent of misdiagnoses. A doctor friend who underwent a brain surgery procedure told me that she received a substantial bill for a fifteen-minute consult with a highly regarded specialist who spent half the time talking about medical salaries. I hope she only paid half the bill . . . for the seven-and-a-half minutes of the medical expertise she actually received!

Although many people feel uncomfortable questioning their doctors, it's essential to be prepared for medical appointments in order to get the best health care results.

UNHAPPY HAGGLER

There seems to be a memo out there that we should always try to "get a better price." For some people, haggling is a game they love to play. A friend of mine told a story about a jacket he saw and instantly wanted. But Al just couldn't bring himself to buy it at full price; he had to offer to pay half the price. The salesman was not biting. Al then offered to pay two-thirds of the price. This went on for enough time that Al dug himself in pretty deeply and the salesman wouldn't budge. His wife just stepped away, as the game of haggling is not her favorite. Finally, Al and his wife walked out of the store. "I really wanted the jacket, but after all my counteroffers, there was no way I could lose face . . . so I had my wife call and order it for me . . . and say it was a gift!" And she paid the full original price! At least the salesperson didn't add in a "you were taxing" fee.

Toni Boyle, author and ghostwriter, has a solution for this potential sticky situation and an answer for those who try to negotiate her fee: "If I could lower my fee, then I wasn't telling you the truth in the first place. Why would you want to work with someone who would do that?"

Negotiation expert Ed Brodow, author of Negotiation Boot Camp (Currency Doubleday, New York, 2006), believes everything is negotiable and we should always ask. If the answer is no, then you can decide your next move. If, unlike Al, you don't have someone who can or will do cleanup detail, you may want to reconsider how you negotiate and whether to play the haggling game.

THE JOB INTERVIEW

One of the most nerve-racking situations is the job interview. Although it varies from company to company, there's always a lot at stake. Being prepared is a must. Do your due diligence on the company and the position to be filled. Have questions ready. Asking about vacations is fair, but it should be one of the last questions posed, not one of the first. This has happened enough in the past few years that articles and commentary about Gen Y/ Millennials giving the impression they aren't hard workers have been published in a variety of sources.

Giving the impression of being foolish, impolitic or just rude can be avoided by turning off phones. Danielle, the director of state libraries, scheduled an interview with a candidate for a library position, who arrived fifteen minutes late. Danielle said, "Partway into the interview, the candidate got a call on her cell phone and answered it. From the sound of the conversation that we all could hear, we knew that it was from a boyfriend. And she stayed on the phone rather than quickly excusing herself and then shutting off the phone. Although she apologized for taking the call, the biggest faux pas she made was saying a swear word that she thought must have been to herself. Everyone on the interview panel heard her. With three strikes against her, she left us no choice but to drop her from our potential employees list." To prevent the sticky face-to-face job interview from going awry, turn off all gadgets and put them away. Focus on the issue at hand. And don't swear, even under your breath.

Although the airwaves, print media and cyberspace are filled with invectives that used to get some of our mouths washed out with soap or get others the less tasty "time-out," curse words do not belong in the face-to-face place. You never know who might find such language off-putting. It could be a boss, customer or potential mentor, and there might be repercussions that aren't worth the word that causes them. You could lose a job, a contract, a referral, a promotion or the respect of others.

The Long and Short of It

Being prepared for any interview can make it go smoothly. Anticipating questions and thinking through and practicing your answers helps. The answers shouldn't be cryptic or long-winded. A friend of mine was interviewing a candidate for a position in a city and county department and said, "I asked him one question, and his answer, the unabridged version, was so detailed and went on for so long, I felt like I had to catch my breath." That's not the best impression to leave. The job candidate should have checked his interviewer's body language for a clue on when to wrap up his answer.

Temper, Temper

We have all encountered people who make snide remarks, proffer an insult or lose their cool and raise their voice as they speak. When in face-to-face situations, dealing with such an outburst is certainly a sticky situation. Rather than escalate the exchange to a shouting match, do the opposite. Speaking more quietly and more calmly than the other person is a tactic I have used. If the other person gets carried away, acknowledge the issue and its import and offer to discuss it at another time: "This seems to be a problem. Let's talk about it another time, after we've given it some thought." The other person may calm down or just agree to discuss it later.

THE PLANE PAIN

Airline travel is more complicated and stressful than it used to be. It's one of the areas where we're in the shared face-to-face space from the moment we enter the airport until we leave our destination airport. This is where it pays to be prepared to meet TSA regulations and be pleasant to airport personnel. The friendly skies are now as fully crowded as are the planes; and air traffic controllers are dealing with fuller commercial schedules and the increase of private jets. These are trying times.

What do you do with the sticky air travel situation? By the way, that means different things to different people. For many, the talkative seatmate is a nightmare; others not. I will often have a short exchange and then politely excuse myself. But the seatmate with the hacking cough is hell to me. Then there was the toddler who threw up on mommy, who was seated next to me, and there wasn't an empty seat I could move to. For the talkative seatmate solution, I've seen passengers immediately put on headphones or use iPod Ear Buds or open their laptops or books. It's best to say, "If you'll excuse me," with a smile and a pleasant tone of voice. No, we don't have to say that . . . but it's kinder if we do.

When there are flight cancellations and delays and other hellish sorts of nightmares wrought by the weather, yelling at the desk personnel is simply not smart, yet I've seen and heard this far too often. One person I know carried on so badly that he landed himself on the airline's "do not fly" list. Airline personnel are the people who can get you out on the next flight or make sure that you don't get on that plane. Human nature being what it is, airline personnel aren't going to be as accommodating to the person berating them as they will be to the pleasant person.

Our encounters with others in the face-to-face space can be sources of inspiration or perspiration. The sweat drops from our brows as we consider how to handle these sticky and oft-complicated situations. Life is full of human encounters that make us think, as well as squirm. But we shouldn't avoid face-to-face situations just because of the 5 percent that may give us pause for thought.

Have a few stock comments in place so that you aren't caught off guard and you're prepared with something to say. Remember: today's sticky situation and annoyance is tomorrow's great story to share. As the ancient Talmud saying goes, "Humor is tragedy plus time." In time, the punch line appears and we get a story to add to our collection and our conversations.

ROANE'S REMINDERS

* How to deal with an offensive comment varies depending on who makes it and where.
* Have several generic remarks in your conversational quiver so that you aren't caught off guard.
* Use "I" messages. "I'm surprised, disappointed, perplexed that you . . ."
* For the consistent One-Upper, bring his behavior to his attention: "I had no idea our vacations (cars, computers, bonuses, sales purchases) were a contest."
* To set boundaries and let people know they've transgressed, do not smile when delivering your comment.
* Saying nothing is only silent approval when also nothing is done.
* "Old school" doesn't permit bad words about good people.
* It's okay to agree to disagree and move on to another subject.

Chapter Fifteen

~~~❧~~~

Techie Toys: Gizmos, Gadgets and Good Behavior

Where to begin? To say that technology and its gizmos and gadgets have rocked our world is an understatement. In so many ways they have made aspects of life easier and more interesting. It's great to be able to see the wedding we couldn't attend, find our long-lost friends, download movies on our iPod, learn about current research on diseases, develop a community of online friends, stay in touch with relatives around the world, give and receive pings (Facebook) and tweets (Twitter) or get stats downloaded off the company database for an important meeting.

The new techie toys continue to impact our face-to-face interactions and add to our list of "must-have cool tools and stuff," which are upgraded every nanosecond. Before we had learned how to set the clock on the VCR, the DVD player became all the rage. And the convenience of being able to tape a favorite TV show seems pale compared to the wonders of TiVo® and DVRs and the ability to watch our favorite shows on our cell phone. By the time we mastered how to set up our blogs, it was time to learn to podcast our messages.

THE DIGITAL DILEMMA

This chapter is the dicey one, because our dependence on those techie gadgets has caused a stir. The evidence is everywhere. Go to a party, meeting, movie, restaurant, school graduation or company retreat and people are multitasking with their techie gadgets. That's another way of saying people are half listening or half paying attention.

Digital tchotchkes have great features and measureless benefits, except that they diminish face-to-face connections, conversations, and collaborations. Most importantly, they are things that should be used in moderation when we're among people. Knowing when, where, and how to navigate these rough waters is the theme of this book as we reclaim and reestablish our interpersonal presence.

LICENSE TO DECIPHER

Much has been written about deciphering text message lingo. Deciphering it is tantamount to decoding personalized license plates. Because mine is "MNGLMVN," I've had conversations with people who have fun figuring out what my license plate means. URGR8 is no different.

Hot Tip

Nearly half the executives in a recent survey said the entry-level (and, I bet, other levels as well) workers lacked writing skills and wrote company e-mails as if texting. Message from employers: Spell your words correctly and in full (Phyllis Korkki, New York Times, August 26, 2007).

Smart texters know that they need to revert to formal English when the situation merits it. Boomers and others who worry about text-message English need to think of it as this generation's Pig Latin or shorthand.

TECHIE KNOW-HOW

As you read this book, there will be newer applications and newer gizmos that we'll embrace and hopefully master. Using these tech-know discoveries and our turning into tech-know-how users is essential. But in this digital whirling world, our professional and personal lives are also served by mastering old-school rules. It's not an either/or; it's a both/and, combining online and face-to-face worlds. The goal is to mix and meld our modes of communication so that our work life and private life benefit from adding our personal touch to this digital world. If everyone else instant messages the person at the next desk, get up, walk over, and talk face to face. Or if everyone is e-mailing potential clients, pick up the phone.

"The online world complements in-person networking and is not a substitute for it," according to Diane K. Danielson, co-author of The Savvy Gal's Guide to Online Networking (or What Would Jane Austen Do? (Booklocker.com, Inc., 2007) and CEO of Downtown WomensClub.com. We have to use offline and online strategies and tools to be effective in today's market-place. If a grandparent or great aunt or customer likes to hear our voice, we do the respectful thing and honor that request, and make a call to that friend or relative or customer who prefers to hear from us.

The best way to find out how the people in our professional and personal lives prefer being contacted is simply to ask. It can be confusing and complicating when someone prefers e-mail only and we have limited access, or someone is a phone person and we're not. But at least then we know the best way to communicate with him or her.

Hot Tip

We have to be sure that our cell phone is turned off when we're face to face with people who deserve our full attention or in public space. We shouldn't put people through our downloaded ringer. It's intrusive and inappropriate. If you expect an urgent call, consider the vibrate mode and inform the person who's with you.

If we forget to turn off our cell phone, the results can be disastrous. Deb, who owns an association management firm, heard from her distraught nephew. As he was interviewing for an important internship, his cell phone made the noise associated with the vibrate mode. It didn't even ring, but the interviewer heard it, stood up, and said the interview was over. To some, that may seem harsh. But if you're interested in hiring the best candidate, the one who forgets his phone is on, or who would even bring it into an interview, is not that person.

While it's also courteous to turn off our cell phone when we're in the public space in the bank, the doctor's office, the post office, or in line at the supermarket, turnabout is fair play. Sergio Paganelli needed a haircut the day his regular stylist was off: "I thought it would be okay to have my hair cut by one of the other people in the shop. She received a call, and rather than take the message and return it later, she held the phone between her chin and shoulder and continued to cut my hair." When I asked him what he said to her, Sergio said he wanted to let her know this was not the way to treat a customer, but he said nothing at the time. I asked him why not. "She held the scissors and the clippers, and I didn't know what she might do to my hair!"

Turning off our cell phone makes business sense and is a nonverbal compliment to the people we're with. The unspoken message is: "You are important." That's the message Tory Johnson gave when we met for coffee. Given her position as CEO of WomenForHire.com and her reporting on Good Morning

America, I wouldn't have thought she would have turned off her phone. I was flattered. Moreover, Tory's thoughtfulness deepened my respect for her.

AVOID BEING A SAP

While the term sap refers to a person who gets taken, my SAP is different. We don't want inappropriate use of our gizmos and gadgets to deliver a damaging message about us. SAP is the person who does the "Sneak A Peak" at his or her BlackBerry or checks messages while in the company of others.

Jobs, contracts, and business deals have been lost due to the SAPpy behavior of otherwise smart people. The Wall Street Journal highlighted a story about a senior executive who was being recruited and interviewed over lunch. When he felt a message appear, he did the SAP at his BlackBerry/Treo and lost the mid-six-figure position.

Psychology Today's "Insights" section on leaders relates that sustained eye contact and big smiles show our charm (March/April 2007, p. 15). If we're looking at our techie gadgets, eye contact has ceased . . . and so has the charm we convey face to face.

A Fine Line

We can make our dinner guests, friends, dates or family feel second best when our text, phone and e-mail messages take preference. "Kathy's" longtime friend was visiting from the East Coast. Because some of the areas of San Mateo County don't have cell phone coverage, she was out of range. "So, you get to check out the scenery instead of your messages," Kathy suggested to her friend.

"We arrived at the seaside restaurant in Half Moon Bay and were seated at the bar. My friend was ecstatic. 'A bar!' she practically shouted. I thought she was impressed with the handcrafted wooden one where we were seated. I did a double take as she was staring at her cell phone and saw bars indicating she finally had reception. She proceeded to check her messages while the bartender tried twice to take our order. While we ate dinner, she pulled out her cell phone to reply to a text from the 'BF' back east. When she hit the ten-minute mark, I almost hit the roof. 'It's a text message, not an epic poem or e-mail. All you had to do is let him know you're at dinner and would get back to him later.'" She crossed the not-so-fine line.

When we're with people, whether we're seated across from them at the dinner table at home or in a restaurant or at a conference table, what we do has as much impact as what we say. Let's make the best impression that builds rapport.

MIND-BLOGGING THOUGHTS

As a blogger since August 2004, I'm a fan of this form of sharing thoughts, information, advice and new ideas. There are several blogs that I visit and have recommended and subscribed to, including that of Guy Kawasaki and Dan Pink. Events motivate me to add an entry to today's version of my "Dear Diary." But, to some, blogs are more like "Dear Diatribe." Do we really want to have everything we think or feel or rant about accessible to others? Like our bosses? Our clients? Our parents? Industry recruiters?

This is a brave new technological world where what we do in cyberspace impacts us across the board and the motherboard (where it all hides, but can be found!).

A RELIGIOUS EXPERIENCE

There's hardly a minister, priest or rabbi who doesn't have a story about a worshipper's cell phone ringing during a solemn service. And now there are stories about grave-site services interrupted by the ringing of the cell phone—carried by the clergy men and women. At a wedding, the rabbi began the ceremony by asking the guests to turn off their cell phones. We then hear a cacophony of contrasting melodies as the guests followed his suggestion.

Many public venues now find it necessary to request that their patrons turn off their cell phones before each performance; that means no texting, as well. And haven't we all been to a movie, theater, or public event at which people took the calls and then chatted noisily? Again, it's the "all-me-all-the-time" gang totally tethered to their digital age, grown-up toys, and disconnected from the common sense of living in a community.

Another distraction is the backlight of the cell phone used to send and receive messages. Most theater productions employ a lighting expert. The backlit phones interfere with the setting and mood of the theater. During the entire performance of Altar Boyz, a young woman in front of me was text messaging, and the backlight interfered with the play's lighting and mood. I've heard the same thing has happened in plays on Broadway and across the country even though announcements are made about turning off the gadgetry. Considering the price we pay for admission, we don't want to have our enjoyment diminished.

To be fair, there are people who ruin the movie, the play or the concert because they're "Old-School Rude." They blithely chat on throughout the event. One associate of mine mentioned that he sat next to a couple who talked throughout the movie. "That's just as annoying as a cell phone conversation." What to do? Saying something directly to the offender can work—or not. The trick is to use a calm tone of voice, be polite and choose your words carefully: "I'm having trouble hearing and would appreciate if you would refrain from talking."

We need to go back to the basic theme: we make the right impression when we're considerate of others when we're in the shared public space—and that includes the use of our techno toys.

WORKPLACE WOES

Using personal cell phones in the workplace can cause other problems. When we take them to client meetings, the sounds of the "William Tell Overture" or "Flight of the Bumblebee" are a disturbance. Even the buzzing sound of the vibrating phone can be an interference, giving the message that our personal phone call is more important than our current business activity. If we're expecting an urgent call or text message, people will understand if we tell them about the situation at the beginning of the gathering, but not if we assume that our cell phone and PDA deserve priority.

It's been interesting to see the cell phones and PDAs attached to biking shorts on the trail, to sweat suits in the gym, and to tuxedo jackets. At a formal dinner a colleague, who had just had a mild heart attack and been told to slow down, showed me the gizmo he wore in the inside pocket of his tux. I just looked at him and shook my head. He'd just had a heart attack! The message he should've gotten is: Lose the gadget. Save your life!

BLUETOOTH® BLUES

Wireless Bluetooth® is a boon to drivers who want to, and must, according to certain state laws, keep their hands on the wheel. In fact, they've become a fashion statement in some arenas. According to Erin Collopy, public relations specialist, when Sean Combs, formerly known as P. Diddy, was seen wearing his Plantronics Bluetooth® headset, the hip-hop world took note: "Several months later, I attended a local music festival and smiled. One of the hip-hop groups was on stage, and during their number they were wearing the Bluetooth model Sean Combs wore as an accessory." Fortunately, none of the entertainers received a call! Maybe Sean Combs will carry around a copy of Face to Face!

The Bluetooth Nonmingling Message

Across the country the message of self-importance is blasting way too loudly. From memorials to family celebrations, we're seeing people turned out in their Bluetooth finery. Really, why on earth would anyone walk into a memorial service in Marin County,

California, or pay a condolence call in Chicago or attend a high school reunion in Roanoke, Virginia, wearing a Bluetooth? The implicit statement is: "I'm self-absorbed." Perhaps people have forgotten they were wearing their ear accessory. But it's not so comfortable as to be easily forgotten.

Hot Tip
Check your ears before you enter the event.

It looks as if no matter what's been said or done to enlighten or discourage them, some people continue to disconnect from their face-to-face conversations. They want to see what "better option" awaits them at the other end of the digital leash that yanks them away with a beep, a tune or a buzz.

Hot Tip
We don't have to give up our techie toys. They're wonderful communication tools. But we have to use them wisely in the "our space" portion of our lives.

The September 2007 issue of Reader's Digest featured an item in its "Life in These United States" section. Lesley Carlon of Bend, Oregon, noticed an interpersonal communication course offered through the community college. But this course on interpersonal skills was "only offered online." Ironic, to be sure. No wonder we're losing our face-to-face communication skills.

THE ROYAL TREATMENT

Kingston Cole, an independent broadband telecommunications consultant, is a man of impeccable manners and the exemplary

Bluetooth user. I bumped into him at the local Trader Joe's. As our conversation continued by the produce section, his hand went up to his ear and he removed the Bluetooth, explaining, "Look, I'm out of the office, so I need to leave my phone on." I understood, as the same applied to me. But I was appreciative, because the thing attached to his ear had been distracting to me—and he had picked up on that. The conversation continued. His decision to remove the Bluetooth made me feel that our exchange was important.

Hot Tip

To make people feel important, follow the Bluetooth "Cole" of Conduct and remove it for the moment.

BLUETOOTH BENEFITS: THE HEAR AND NOW

There's a wonderful serendipitous benefit to the invention and use of wireless Bluetooth. Because it's an accepted and often needed accessory, some hearing aids have been redesigned that resemble the Bluetooth model. When I first saw the ad, I had to reread it to be sure it was a hearing device. And it was. As our population gets older and the younger demographic blasts their music in their Ear Buds, the increase of those with hearing loss grows. If people actually wear these hearing aids because they now look cooler, that's good news. Preventing the possible need for a hearing aid is an even better idea.

Sadly, the studies on the dangers of iPod and MP3 Ear Buds or even headphones blasting music have been the topic of current research. Audiological studies on the impact of loud rock music have occurred since the late '60s. Conclusion: Don't risk your hearing health by blasting your eardrums.

Hot Tip

Beware of wearing your iPod or MP3 Ear Buds in the face-to-face space when you're with people. Doing so sends out a message: "I'm completely disinterested in you and whatever you have to say." Using them on a subway, in the gym or in an airport when you're alone is fine. Avoid wearing them at a conference, reception, seminar, meeting or party.

SAD TRUTH IN SAN FRANCISCO

In the recent past, a young woman was the victim of a hit-and-run. In every article covering this horrific murder, it mentioned she was running in the Presidio wearing her iPod. Her "peripheral hearing" was blocked, and she never heard the car driving behind her. It was dark at 6:30 A.M., and apparently the driver didn't see her. It was a senseless loss of a young woman with a bright future. I include this story as a cautionary tale. While MP3 players are great, anything that blocks our hearing can be a problem. We must be careful how we use these gadgets in the open space or anyplace where there is traffic.

E-MAIL-STROM

Everybody and their grandmother e-mails, and that's good. We can stay in touch with the office, colleagues, friends, siblings, offspring, and clients for the cost of a local call. Some busy people still send out group "here's what I've been up to" e-mails, almost like mini-newsletters or the holiday letter that some people find impersonal and annoying. Others understand twenty-first-century hectic lifestyles and appreciate the effort, however minimal, to keep friends updated. And some people understand that the message written on a card is the essence of their personal touch.

An attorney friend of several decades sent only group e-mails for over three years. That strikes me the same as the preprinted holiday card with not one personal word or a written signature— worthless. All it shows is that I made a list serve that serves the sender, not the recipient. Sad to say, my cards, individual e-mails and calls were not returned. It may have taken me a while, but I finally got the message.

Unfortunately, some of us use e-mail to convey messages that should be done verbally, because it's easier to face the screen and type than face a person and speak. Just because it's easy, doesn't make it right! Although we can send them electronically, there are some things that aren't best served by e-mail or text message and should be avoided. These include:

1. The "Dear John or Jeanette" letter ending a relationship
2. The breakup announcement to family and friends
3. The wedding invitation
4. The thank-you note for the wedding, graduation, or special occasion gift
5. The "pink slip"

The first message of condolence or sympathy can be sent via e-mail so that there's an immediate message of sympathy. Following it up with a sympathy card will offer additional, even long-term, comfort to the bereaved. The phone call is also a nice personal touch.

A number of major newspapers are part of Legacy.com, based on their obituary sections. People can post words of support for the bereaved family. The Chicago Sun Times and Chicago Tribune did that for my mother, and we found the lovely stories and thoughts from across North America to be consoling. But we saved the notes and cards.

The all-time low in the acknowledgement department was reported in a paper when the bride and groom sent a group e-mail thank-you to all their wired guests. This, sadly, is not a one-time phenomenon. Oh, yes, it saves time and the money for note cards, ink and stamps. Hopefully, it saves all of the guests from buying any future presents for this couple. In this technology-saturated time, we need more than ever to maintain our personal touch and our good manners. If people take the time to choose, buy, send or bring a gift as a response to a celebratory invitation, surely the recipients can make the time to put pen to paper and express appreciation.

Hot Tip

If you've sent an e-mail that merits a reply but haven't received one, pick up the phone. Some e-mails get lost in cyberspace and don't bounce back to the sender. We can't assume cyberspace has a perfect delivery track record. With so many junk mail filters, our non-junk e-mail can be misfiled. The twenty-first century has given a whole new twist to the famous guilt trip line, "You never call or write anymore." We need to pick up the phone and have a simultaneous interaction instead of just a "screen gem."

Court-ing E-mail Disaster

E-mails are admissible in courts of law, be they criminal, civil, divorce or Supreme. Whether it's the New York Times firing a number of employees for forwarding inappropriate e-mails, the infamous Enron case, the Justice Department reviewing e-mails as part of insider trading or the retrieving of the outgoing e-mails off a suspect's server, we need to be judicious about the e-mails we send. Even Microsoft's techno-wizard, Bill Gates, couldn't eradicate what had been written in e-mails. In their quiet, high-tech way, e-mails may become the Rosetta Stones of our age.

Careers have been damaged and marriages destroyed by hitting the send button. Friendships and business relationships have been altered by the e-mail that has no tone, inflection, or facial cues to impact the intent of the words. I learned this the hard way when I received an e-mail that sounded mean-spirited when read without benefit of human interaction. The same message delivered fact to face or by phone might have sounded different and not been painful to receive. Now, when I have something difficult to impart or dicey to deal with, I think of the impact of my communication before I hit send, and then I pick up the phone instead. That way, tone, intent, inflection and humor can be heard, and we may avoid unintentionally insulting someone. Saving a relationship with a client, colleague or friend is worth the effort.

It's better to leave a voice mail—not the way-too-long "voice novel"—that can be heard correctly than send an e-mail that can be misinterpreted, thereby sending the wrong message.

Baby News

We really need to think before we send. Jennifer Walker e-mailed a longtime friend to let her know she and her husband were expecting again. Jennifer had first left a message, but not hearing back, she thought her friend might have been on vacation. In her e-mail, Jennifer let her friend know the due date, how much she liked her doctor and the new type of sonogram confirming the viability of the pregnancy at six weeks.

The e-mail she received back was shocking: "Just remember, you're not out of the woods yet." Technically, no mom is out of the woods until the baby is delivered. But receiving this thoughtless, inappropriate e-mail was more than hurtful. There are some things that shouldn't be sent or said! This had to be an infamous example. Just because we think or know something does not mean it has to be vocalized or written.

Memo Madness

In more than one corporate office, the use of e-mail has escalated to "Memo Wars." A New York consultant with a major firm told me, "It's unbelievable how much time we waste writing two- or three-page e-mail memos and then copying everyone to justify a comment, action or decision. The e-mails shoot back and forth and involve far too many people. Isn't it smarter to get up from your computer, walk across the hall, and talk about the issue?"

Rosie Amodio, who was then editor at TheKnot.com, always has known the value of face-to-face conversation in the office: "I get up from my chair and walk over to the desk of an assistant editor to make a request or suggestion. It seems that most of our younger editors only e-mail. Some days I might be the only person who actually talks to them, asks how they are, catches up a bit and makes my request or comment nicely and face to face. The responses are always positive." Rosie, now an editor at In Style, is part of the digital, wired world and also brings her personal touch to her workplace.

Fwd: Person

The growing rate of unnecessary e-mail is annoying. In this case, I'm not talking about spam, that unsolicited and unwanted advertising mail that swamps our inboxes. I'm referring to the mail from people we know who send on their idea of funny jokes, important warnings, and poignant poems with a six-screen list of other recipients' names. It makes an impression—one that says, "We don't know how to use this technological game of buzz."

One way to handle the "fwd: person" is to ask him or her to stop. Suzanne Haring, a New York party entertainer, sent out what she calls an official "Forwarding Moratorium," asking people not to forward things, as she doesn't have the time, the inclination, and sometimes the e-mail box space to handle them all. She has had to send the moratorium more than once because the "It's-All-About-Me-All-the-Timers" paid no attention to her request. Maybe they were so busy sending other forwarded e-mails that they didn't have time to read hers!

How we word these requests is important. I just sent a long-time friend (since grammar school) an e-mail that said I so enjoy seeing her e-mail in my inbox, but I'd much prefer to read how and what she's doing. Some may find that to be too wishy-washy, but I only want the deluge of forwarded e-mails to stop, not our friendship. So, until she gets that hint, I'll continue to delete the fwd: group e-mail rather than make a big deal out of it.

Being adept at the use of technology helps us manage our careers, businesses and lives. When we do so in a way that is considerate of others, we make the right impression in the face-to-face space.

BLACK-BURY OUR ADDICTION

The PDA is a boon to the boondoggle of staying connected. Whether it's Research in Motion's BlackBerry, Palm's Treo or the new Web-enabled super Wii-Fi phones, we can receive and send messages 24/7 without carrying a laptop. Each generation of these techno-wonders has new applications that are awesome.

The ability to log into my Treo™ anywhere anytime has been an enormous help to my speaking business and authorial life. I can check my e-mail as I sit in the cafe writing and handle business in a timely fashion. Even the camera—something I was sure I would never use—has proven useful. But overuse, misuse and abuse of these gadgets and their addictive nature have provided fodder for articles, blogs, and face-to-face conversations.

Wait, let me rephrase that—BlackBerrys are inanimate objects and do not have an addictive nature. Wake-up call: they are not the addicts; we are! So now we can join a twelve-step (make it six, as we're too busy for twelve) program.

GADGETRI-AGE

I couldn't resist the wordplay on triage. Our techie toys can cause medical problems. According to Newsweek (July 27, 2007, p. 58), the smaller the devices, the more prone we are to injuries: "The American Physical Therapy Association warned that frequent users of BlackBerry-type devices are more likely to experience swelling and tendonitis." Several spas have started to offer BlackBerry massages for their digitally adept clients' digits. There's also the potential for neck strain from misuse of laptops. And the New England Journal of Medicine reported that a medical student, Julio Bonis, diagnosed himself with "acute Wii-Fi-itis" after ten hours of virtual tennis! I wonder what Roger Federer would suggest.

Earlier in the book, I suggested that we not use these techno-gadgets in certain public spaces, and I included restrooms for good reason. Mike Carruthers, longtime radio personality and host of the syndicated program Something You Should Know, attended a radio industry conference in Santa Monica: "I went into the men's room and witnessed something that left me speechless. I was using the middle urinal and noticed that the guys on each side of me were multitasking—they were using the urinals while they talked on their cell phones! I remember thinking, 'These guys must be important, because I can't imagine a call so urgent it can't wait.'" (Sorry, dear readers, but we decided there would be no graphic or cartoon illustrating these multitasking men!)

FAMILY AND FRIEND SPACE

Let's get practical. The time we need to check our phone and PDA for business messages is far less often than we think. If we're in shared space with family, colleagues and friends, the uber-message we're giving is: "You're not as important or interesting as what might appear in my inbox."

Instead of multitasking, let's try single-tasking and focus on the company, the conversation and the food. Check your cell phone or PDA later. You'll make your companions feel important because they'll have received something very precious: your undivided attention. What better personal touch?

ROANE'S REMINDERS

* Technology enhances face-to-face communication but is not a substitute for it.
* Know when to use the phone appropriately to convey a message.

* Cell phones will draw people together and give them a reason to disconnect as well.
* Learn to cut-and-paste e-mail to eliminate multiple screens of forwarded names.
* Only forward funny, touching, or motivating e-mails when you're sure they're welcomed.
* Do not use e-mails to break up, fire, give bad news, or acknowledge wedding gifts.
* Know the time and place for using gizmos and gadgets in the public and social space.
* Remove the Bluetooth before entering a gathering.

Chapter Sixteen

Route 66: Face-to-Face Steps to Success

Based on the iconic cross-country highway that has been immortalized in song (You can get your kicks on Route 66), this chapter summarizes the best behaviors, actions and attitudes to master for face-to-face encounters and experiences, and how to make the most of interpersonal communication. It also doubles as a checklist of what to do and what not to do to create a great reputation; weave a web of colleagues, coworkers, clients and cronies; and make lifelong friends along the highway of life.

1. Acknowledge gifts, leads, information, ideas and support (e-mail first or call, and follow up with handwritten notes).
2. Stay in touch with people even when you need nothing (by e-mail, text and instant messages, phone and snail mail).
3. Identify both your offline and online network.
4. "Lower the ladder" to bring up the next generation.
5. Keep people in the loop about leads, projects and contracts.
6. Treat people as people, not as prospects.
7. Make people feel comfortable with you.
8. Don't confuse conversations with grilling (avoid asking too many questions).
9. Have good manners; know etiquette, net-iquette, and text-iquette.
10. Treat people kindly and with an Aretha dose of RESPECT.
11. Treat people the way they want to be treated.
12. Take responsibility: "My error—how can we remedy this?"
13. Apologize when in error. ("My Bad" is not an apology.)
14. Be a matchmaker: connect people with jobs, clients and resources.

15. Avoid "attachment disorder" (sending unnecessary e-mail attachments).
16. Volunteer in the community.
17. Respect privacy and property.
18. Work hard and smart, and do a great job.
19. Take time to smell the roses.
20. Develop a sense of timing.
21. Be connected—not tethered to technology.
22. Respect others when using cell phones, iPods, and PDAs in "our" space (that means not in theaters, meetings, restaurants, elevators, parties, houses of worship or on dates).
23. Pay attention to people when they're talking to you.
24. Embrace diversity of age, race, religion, expertise and cultures.
25. Stay visible, especially in professional organizations.
26. Honor people's time.
27. Be approachable, inclusive and tactful.
28. Refrain from FF—Foolish Forwarding—of e-mail, jokes, videos . . . unless you have permission to do so.
29. Be of good humor.
30. Know how to work rooms.
31. Pick up the phone to connect.
32. Remember your roots.
33. Praise and support others.
34. Ask for help.
35. Offer assistance.
36. Don't make snap judgements.
37. Be guided by goals, not blinded by them.
38. Refrain from offering unsolicited opinions! (Corollary: There is no such thing as "constructive criticism.")
39. Give credit where credit is due (for ideas, projects, and funny comments). Always attribute.
40. Express appreciation and give recognition. "Thank you" is a powerful phrase.
41. Offer and collect business cards with grace.
42. Connect, communicate, engage and collaborate.

43. Pass on third-party praise to the proper recipient . . . in front of others.
44. Give sincere compliments.
45. Accept compliments graciously.
46. Avoid malicious gossip and rumors.
47. Be a lifelong learner.
48. "Make nice" in the rooms you work and work in.
49. Listen, listen, listen!
50. Be generous of spirit.
51. Do what you say you'll do—when you say you'll do it!
52. Know when to hold 'em and when to fold 'em. Exit graciously.
53. Avoid exaggeration and embellishment.
54. Forget about using text-message English in workplace e-mails.
55. Hang around with the people who inspire.
56. Give people a second chance.
57. Avoid using humor as a guise for put-downs.
58. Avoid e-mail or text messages to fire or breakup or deliver other unpleasant news.
59. Don't leave people dangling.
60. Mentor the next generation (or the prior one).
61. Control your temper—use only "I" messages when giving feedback.
62. Be easy to be around.
63. Do good deeds.
64. Be a person of exemplary character—the one who would make your favorite grandparent proud.
65. Be a good friend.
66. Have fun!

As you travel along your journey, if you embrace these simple, easy-to-implement actions, strategies and ideas, you won't go wrong. You'll have successful interactions that will speed you along and improve your face-to-face communication professionally and personally.

RECOMMENDED READING

Barabasi, Alberto-Laszlo, Ph.D. *Linked*. Perseus, Cambridge, MA, 2002.

Black, Joanne. *No More Cold Calling*™. Warner Business Books, New York, NY, 2006.

Briles, Judith, Ph.D. *Woman to Woman 2000: Becoming Sabotage Savvy in the New Millennium*. New Horizon Press, Far Hills, NJ, 2000.

Brodow, Ed. *Negotiation Boot Camp*™. Currency, New York, NY, 2006.

Carducci, Bernardo. *Shyness, A Bold Approach*. HarperCollins, New York, NY, 1999.

Epstein, Joseph. *Snobbery*. Houghton Mifflin, New York, NY, 2006.

Glaser, Connie. *Gender Talk Works*. Windsor Works Hall Press, Atlanta, GA, 2006.

Heath, Chip and Dan. *Made to Stick*. Random House, New York, NY, 2007.

Kawasaki, Guy. *Art of the Start*. Penguin USA. New York, NY, 2004.

Lancaster, Lynne C., Stillman, David. *When Generations Collide*. HarperCollins, New York, NY, 2002.

Misner, Ivan PHD *Masters of Success*. McGraw-Hill, New York, NY, 2007.

Pink, Daniel. *A Whole New Mind*. Riverbird Books, New York, NY, 2006.

RoAne, Susan. *How To Work A Room*®. Collins, New York, NY, 2007

RoAne, Susan. *How to Create Your Own Luck*. Wiley and Sons, Hoboken, NJ, 2004.

AFTERWORD

Life is not about my space or your space. It's about *our* space and how we inhabit and behave in shared areas of our lives.

My goal was to write a book that's a practical guide to navigating those times when we're face to face with people who cross our proverbial and real paths.

May you reap the benefits and rewards that face-to-face opportunities provide. I hope it's an e-ticket (Disneyland-style) ride.

Thank you for reading *Face to Face*.

ROANE'S READERS' GUIDE TO FACE TO FACE

The following questions are offered to stimulate a discussion about why and how to increase our face-to-face interactions and add the personal touch to our digital world. This readers' guide can be used by a company team, a workplace book group as a discussion forum, or as part of a university class as have my other books, which are the perfect offline face-to-face settings to talk about . . . face-to-face conversations, connections and interactions.

If you have questions or ideas for me, please e-mail:

info@face2facebook.com

or visit

www.face2facebook.com

or

www.susanroane.com.

1. What would be the benefits to you of being comfortable and facile in face-to-face situations?
2. What type of face-to-face situations do you encounter in your work life? Personal life?
3. What is your attitude about small talk?
4. Discuss any instances where small talk led to something *bigger*.
5. What do you do to prepare for business events? Social events?
6. What's the most interesting outcome you've had from a face-to-face interaction, whether at an event, meeting or in the office?
7. Do you consider yourself shy? If yes, in what types of situations?
8. What do you do to make yourself more confident to neutralize your shyness?
9. Name five people in your sphere who are Talk Targets. What do they do to encourage communication?

10. Are there any tips you can borrow from them?
11. When was the last time you invited a coworker or colleague to lunch? The results? (i.e., shared information, common interests, work-related issues, just plain fun)
12. What's the best way you've found to handle the "pick up the tab" issue?
13. Are you privy to much of the office "news"? Was there an office circumstance that surprised you?
14. How do you stay "in the know"?
15. How often do you stay in touch with your network? How?
16. Did your cell phone ever ring at a "bad" time? How did you handle that?
17. What are your phone pet peeves?
18. What are your experiences where communication was helped or hindered by e-mail/texting?
19. Are there any situations that you resolved by a phone conversation that started as an e-mail exchange? What were they?
20. What's the best way you've found to end a phone conversation?
21. How do you begin a conversation with someone you don't know?
22. What is the best experience you had turning a *cold* call into a *warm* one? How did you do that?
23. Would you describe your workplace/team as diverse? How do they work together?
24. What do you do to make others more comfortable with you? The results?
25. Are you part of online social and/or business networks? Which ones? How are they helpful?
26. Would you be interested in having a face-to-face gathering of your online group? How would you go about arranging it?
27. What groups/associations do you belong to? How have they been beneficial? How are you active?
28. Are there groups you want to explore? Why?
29. What was the best toast you've heard (or given)? What made it so?
30. As a member of the audience, do you have any recommendations for people who have to make a presentation?

31. What was the most uncomfortable ending you've initiated? What would you do differently?
32. Have you had a memorable mentor? How did you meet him or her? What is your relationship now?
33. What are your best tips for people who want to know what's going on (informal information) but want to avoid involvement with the office gossipers?
34. What are the sticky situations you've encountered? How did you resolve them?
35. When was the most embarrassing/outrageous time you've seen someone use his or her cell phone or PDA to call or text?
36. What was your funniest face-to-face situation? The results?

There are no right or wrong answers—just comments, situations and your experiences that contribute to face-to-face discussions.

FOR THOSE DESPERATELY
SEEKING SUSAN

. . . a speech is within your reach!

If you want to book bestselling author and in-demand **keynote speaker** Susan RoAne for your meeting, retreat or convention:

Call: 415/461-3915
E-mail: Susan@SusanRoAne.com
Mail: The RoAne Group
320 Via Casitas, Suite 310
Greenbrae, CA 94904
Fax: 415/461-6172
Visit: **www.susanroane.com**

To purchase Susan's print books and audio books:
Visit your local bookstore or online bookstore
Call 1-800-CEO-READ for bulk orders
How to Work a Room®
The Secrets of Savvy Networking
What Do I Say Next?
RoAne's Rules: How to Make the Right Impression
How to Create Your Own Luck
Face to Face

A popular speaker, Susan lectures to corporations, associations and universities on interpersonal communication and savvy networking to build long-lasting business and personal relationships.

INDEX